Provision
In
Unexpected Places

LAURA GAGNON

Copyright © 2017 Laura Gagnon

All rights reserved.

ISBN: 1976099455
ISBN-13: 978-1976099458

Copyright Information

This book or parts thereof may not be reproduced in any form, stored in a retrieval systems, or transmitted in any form by any means – electronic, mechanical, photocopy, recording or otherwise – without prior written permission of the author, except by United States of America Copyright law.

Scripture quotations marked NKJV are from the New King James Version, Copyright © 1982 by Thomas Nelson. Used by permission. All rights reserved.

Scripture quotations marked AMP are from the Amplified Bible, Copyright © 19541964, 1987 by the Lockman Foundation. Used by permission.

Scripture quotations marked MSG are from The Message: The Bible in Contemporary English, Copyright © 1993, 1994, 1995, 1996, 2000, 2001, 2002. Used by permission of NavPress Publishing Corp.

Scripture quotations marked NIV are from the Holy Bible, New International Version, Copyright ©1973, 1978, 1984, 2011 by Biblica, Inc. Used by permission of Zondervan. All rights reserved worldwide, www.zondervan.com. The NIV and New International Version are trademarks registered in the United States Patent and Trademark Office by Biblica, Inc.

Scripture translations marked NLT are from the Holy Bible, New Living Translation, Copyright © 1996, 2004, 2007. Used by permission of Tyndale House Publishers, Inc, Wheaton IL 60189. All rights reserved.

Scripture translations marked VOICE taken from the Voice Bible Copyright © 2012 Thomas Nelson, Inc., Ecclesia Bible Society.

LAURA GAGNON

DEDICATION

To our children: Jon, Jennifer, James, Jessica, Talia & Jace. May these stories inspire your faith and assure your hearts with confidence towards God all the days of your life.

CONTENTS

1	Christ Is In Your Crisis	Pg 1
2	He Knows Me	Pg 15
3	Beyond Our Understanding	Pg 23
4	Just Enough	Pg 35
5	Divine Connections	Pg 42
6	Doors in Unexpected Places	Pg 60
7	Hidden Treasure	Pg 65
8	Accessing God's Strategies	Pg 71
9	Shattering Religious Misconceptions	Pg 78
10	Prayers and Declarations	Pg 85

CHAPTER 1
CHRIST IS IN YOUR CRISIS

One of the most heartbreaking trials anyone can endure in life is the experience of great loss. Every time we turn on the news we see nations in crisis. The things that people have put their security into such as homes, jobs, businesses, bank accounts, government and relationships are being shaken. Multitudes of people are displaced from their homes through massive floods, fires, hurricanes and other natural disasters. The fear and insecurity that people face in light of these types of situations can be enormous. Some people find themselves starting over in an unfamiliar place. It's in that place of disappointment, when you're trying to pick up the pieces, that you are faced with some major decisions. There is a quote by Socrates that puts things in perspective. **"The secret of change is to focus all of your energy, not on fighting the old, but on building the new."**

This book is a collection of stories from our lives, sharing accounts of how God met us in some of our most difficult circumstances. There is a scripture in Psalm 37:25 that says, "I was young and now I am old, yet I have never seen the righteous forsaken or their children begging bread." God has proven His word is true through some times of extreme hardship and uncertainty.

There are many books on Biblical principles of overcoming poverty and supernatural supply, but this book is unique to our personal journey. Although there are Biblical principles woven throughout, it's more about giving hope so that people can learn to trust Him. If someone can discover who God is during their deepest time of need, their relationship with Him will stabilize every other part of their life. Faith will grow exponentially and produce bigger and bigger miracles, until they realize truly nothing is impossible with God! So, please allow me to introduce you to the God that will walk through every trial with you and prove to you, personally, that His word is true.

There will be times in the days ahead when you may find yourself faced with difficulties that you had never imagined, but there is a heavenly Father that will never leave you or forsake you. No matter what you need, it is available to you. Through these stories, we believe others can gain a sense of hope and peace that God is watching out for them. Testimonies of God's faithfulness bring comfort. Nothing catches Him off guard! We can feel reassured that He has already lined up the provision we need. It doesn't matter if the need presents itself today, a month from now or another time in the future. Our Father has earmarked certain things that are just for us, but it's faith in Him that allows us to access what exists in the kingdom of God. Let these testimonies of His love and faithfulness inspire you to believe for your own situations. Faith is the currency of the kingdom of God!

Many years ago, my husband and I endured a very difficult time in our lives. We were both employed with the church we attended, and all our relationships centered around those in the church. Multiple things occurred over a long period of time, and eventually they culminated into some very painful events. The day finally came where we knew it had reached the end. We found ourselves cut off from everyone we knew, and when that door closed we lost everything that we viewed as a source of comfort and security. We lost employment, references and friends. Within 8 months the home we had been renting was sold, forcing us to go a different direction. As that door closed, we realized that we were also being uprooted from the city that had been our home for a long time. It was a very unstable time for us, and the instability led to a great deal of fear.

It took many months to process all the reasons why God had closed those doors. The enemy definitely played a part in all of that, but so did the Lord. He removed us from a very toxic and unhealthy environment, and it was a tremendously painful time in our lives. I felt like every hope for the future had been shattered. What was worse was the fact that my faith in God had been shattered at the same time. He worked in ways that I couldn't understand, and quite honestly, I was so mad and disappointed in Him, ourselves and others that I couldn't understand a lot of it until much later, but those relationships and spiritual ties were killing our faith. All I could do was stuff my grief deep inside, and when I wasn't crying, I was on this horrible roller coaster of emotions. I was angry one moment and deeply depressed the next. Every time I tried to pray, the only thing that came out of my mouth was raw emotion. It didn't make for a great prayer life, and there were many times when I wasn't sure if God was still listening.

Maybe you're in that place now, and you're not sure if you can trust God. Maybe you're in a place where you feel like you don't have a friend in the world to talk to who would really care what you're going through, or perhaps you are struggling with whether or not it's worth it to even whisper a prayer under your breath. My hope in writing this book is that you will allow our stories to quiet your fears. Let me assure you that God truly does care about you!

Our heavenly Father understands that people fail to meet His standard of holiness on a daily basis, but He still longs to have a personal relationship with us. We don't have to be intimidated by a sense of unworthiness because Jesus took care of our sin issue. Misunderstanding the nature and mercy of God causes multitudes of people to develop misconceptions about Him. These distorted perspectives of truth create lies in a person's belief system, producing estrangement, anger, resentment and a sense of abandonment. I wrestled with all of those things. I think part of the reason was due to generational brokenness. Our family struggled with poverty, hardship, parental abandonment and other generational curses that left an imprint of brokenness, bitterness and disappointment in our family line. Those things serve to distort a person's understanding of their heavenly Father.

People experience loss for a variety of reasons. Sometimes we find ourselves in circumstances beyond our control. When life takes unexpected twists and turns, it can cause us to feel helpless to bring about the change we hope will bring us back to a place of stability. This awkward, uncomfortable place is known as **transition.** You can't go back to where you were, and you can feel stuck not knowing how to move forward. If a person isn't careful, fear and anxiety can cause emotional paralysis. Every person, at some point in their life, needs to discover the God that is bigger than dead ends, disasters and difficulty. If we don't, then our impression of God will only ever reach the size of our previous experiences. Until we do, we cannot really experience Him in ways that build our confidence.

When we found ourselves in transition, we both had to deal with a great deal of fear and insecurity about our future. One thing we knew is that we did not want to place any limitations on God or our expectations of how He chose to work in our lives.

The joy of being free from all the strife and toxicity of our former environment was a huge weight off of both of us, but there was also an enormous amount of fear and anxiety over our future. Norm got the idea to write a letter to the landlord to the home we were renting, asking if there was a possibility to work off the rent doing repairs or other jobs. I honestly had no faith for that at all. I was even more surprised when the landlord called and said yes! The home had been badly in need of repairs, but we learned that this couple also had many other properties. They were looking for someone to help with maintenance and repairs on their other properties, and as it turned out, Norm sent the letter at just the right time. These same people eventually asked if we would be willing to relocate to Florida to work on another property they owned that had been damaged by the frequent hurricanes. At the time, it was the only door open. The house we had been renting had already been sold, so we didn't have much of a choice. We drove into Florida while everyone else was evacuating due to Hurricane Ivan.

We landed in a little town called Milton, Florida. Milton felt like it was a dying town, and that was before the hurricane hit. The good news was a local grocery store known as the Pic-N-Save, where it was still possible to buy a week's worth of groceries for next to nothing. That little market was truly a blessing!

We found ourselves in a place where we had no one else to lean on except God. It can be easy to think you know Him until you are left without all your crutches and no safety net. He literally picked us up and transplanted us into a brand new place where we had no relationships outside of Him. We had nothing we could place our security in outside of God.

The fear and insecurity felt like a noose around my neck. Some days I felt like I needed to remind myself, "Just breathe." I would go for a walk down the country roads and hear absolutely nothing. No cars. No planes. No sirens. On some days, there wasn't even the sound of other people. Lots of frogs and crickets, but that was about it. Occasionally, there would be a dog barking in the distance.. After being accustomed to the fast paced city life, it was very difficult to adjust to the slow pace of our new environment. The silence was deafening! At night, I would look up at the stars and think how clear the sky was, and I wondered why I had never paid attention to them. It was so hard for me to find that internal place of peace and rest. God knew we needed it, but I have never been very good at being relaxed. I prefer tightly wound, thank you. That I can do! I was so used to being stressed out I didn't know how to slow down and just experience the peace that was there. God dumped us in a town that was 25 years behind the times. I felt like I was going stir crazy! How would we build a new life in this stifling, backwards little town that time forgot? We both had so many questions and no one to turn to for help, but God was with us, and He became our everything. God used a personal crisis to draw us closer to Him. It was His love that put us in an environment where our faith could grow.

When a person is going through transition, what they really need is hope. They need a light at the end of the tunnel. They need to be encouraged by the testimonies of other people who have gone through something similar, because they need to cling to the hope that God can get them through their own difficulties. The wonderful thing about Him is that His provision is not just in practical things, such as food, shelter or finances. His tender concern towards His children is to provide relief from emotional pain, insecurity, fear and worry. We have a loving Father that knows how to encourage us even on our worst days. God has gotten us through, and He can do it for you, too!

During those days it seemed that God would let us get down to our very last dollar before He would release provision. Sometimes we had less than that. Every time our food or gas began to get low the anxiety would creep up. Oh, how I hated that feeling! I would have to talk myself off of a cliff every single week, reminding myself that God knew our needs and He would take care of us.

When you're going through a difficult time, one of the best ways to encourage your faith is to stop what you're doing and try to remember all the times in the past when God has met your needs. If you don't have any personal history with God of your own, then try to recall other people's testimonies, because if He helped someone else, you know that His help is available for you, too.

One time when I had a serious need for God's intervention, I remembered a story my mother told me a long, long time ago about her grandmother. I never met my great grandmother. About the only thing I knew about her was the fact that she raised my mother, she was a Methodist, and her name was Matilda. My mother told me that her family was quite poor, partly because she was raised during the depression, and partly because her grandmother was widowed and lost her source of income when her husband died. One day, there was no food in the house and Matilda was frantically calling on the name of the Lord in prayer. She would pray and pace, pray and pace, then occasionally go check the pantry simply out of desperation. Finally, after repeating this process nearly all day, she went back to the pantry one last time, and her miracle was sitting right there on the pantry shelf! It was a Mason jar full of navy beans. It's odd to think that something so small and ordinary could be someone's miracle, but for Matilda, it was that day! Although I never knew her personally, one thing stuck with me: I had a great grandmother that knew to call on the name of Jesus, and her faith had caused her to experience at least one miracle in her life.

Sometimes all you need is one testimony to lift your faith, and inspire you to not give up. Sometimes all you need is one testimony to jump start your faith and elevate your prayer life! What testimony has God given you, to remind you that He is a good and faithful friend? It is a tremendous inheritance when God has given you ancestors that dug the wells of prayer for their family. Have you taken the time to ask your parents and grandparents to share their stories of faith? Re-dig those wells and stir up the gift of faith! It lives inside of you! My great grandmother had one of those days where she couldn't afford to take no for an answer, so she kept pressing God to do something for her. When she pressed God to send back an answer, it was her faith that pulled provision out of the unseen realm. Never let the enemy convince you that the miracle isn't in the house, because the miracle is in you. It's that little seed of faith that is growing inside of you, and it is powerful enough to create the miracle you need! That is supernatural faith at work. It is a spiritual legacy that can be passed down from generation to generation. If you want your children to have faith, remind them of God's faithfulness to your family!

God has given each one of us a tiny seed of faith. All of God's promises come in seed form. Faith comes as a seed. If we want to be able to pull miracles out of the kingdom of God, then we must learn to grow our faith. Faith is like a spiritual muscle that needs to exercised. If we don't exercise it, then it won't grow. God knows this, so He gives us opportunities to exercise our faith. It's when the rubber meets the road; everything we think we know about God is put to the test. Desperation brings people to a point of decision, where they have to decide what they believe about God. Desperation causes us to press into the anointing where we have access to God's promises. Jesus is His name, but the word Christ means 'anointed one.' When we bring our urgent requests to Him and insist that He do something for us, we are pulling on Him until His power is released.

There is a story in the Bible about a woman with an issue of blood, and she knew how to pull on Jesus to get what she needed. She was desperate to receive her healing. She struggled with her infirmity for years, spending all that she had on doctors. No matter what she tried, nothing could cure her. Scripture says she followed Jesus until she got close enough to touch Him. She pressed through the crowd because she knew in her heart that if she could just touch Him she would be made well. Jesus, feeling power go out from Him, remarked, "Who touched me?"[1]

Sometimes we just need to keep following Jesus until we get close enough to grab Him and say, "I won't let go until I get what I need!" Jesus knew full well who touched Him, but I believe He asked that question to draw her out of the crowd. Once He did, she felt compelled to explain why she was so desperate, and she acknowledged her desire to be healed. Jesus wouldn't let her feel insignificant any longer. He wouldn't let her be pushed out of the way by the hard-hearted religious crowd., who had shunned her and treated her like an outcast. Jesus wanted more for her than just a physical healing; *He wanted to make her whole.* She would have been content to shrink back into the shadows of obscurity, but He insisted on a personal encounter so that she could look at Him face to face.

---

[1] Luke 8:43-48 The VOICE

When she met his gaze, she discovered the warmth of His smile - a memorable experience that she would remember for the rest of her life. This is the love and kindness that He longs to share with each of us.

God has endless ways of providing. We just need to believe that He wants to help us. One time we received an unexpected refund from an overpayment on a closed credit card account. The overpayment had taken place over a year before and the company sent it to us without us even knowing the overpayment existed. It was over $600! When that check arrived in the mail it was truly a surprise!

Another time, I was in panic mode looking at the empty pantry shelves and wondering how I was going to feed us. I got very good at making something out of very little, but that day there just wasn't anything in the cupboard. I was busy reminding God that it was His job to take care of us when there was a knock at the door. A man from a few houses down wanted to borrow a ladder. He offered to pay us $10 to rent it for the day, and I went down to the Pic-N-Save and got a little food.

Looking at the empty pantry reminded me of the story of a woman in the Bible who faced a similar situation. The prophet, Elijah, had sat by a creek in the wilderness for several years. His sole purpose during this time seemed to just simply wait on God.

Meanwhile, his source of provision slowly dried up. As he was wondering how to tap into the provision God had for him, God instructed him to go to the most unlikely place. There was a woman in a town called Zarephath who was so broke and desperate she was literally starving to death. She had decided to take the last little bit of flour and oil she had and make a small cake for her and her son to eat, then they would lay down and die. THIS is the person God sent his prophet to – a suicidal woman on the brink of hopelessness and despair!

Sometimes there is a storm in our life that picks us up and transports us to a new place because we are the answer to someone else's prayer. This was true in Elijah's case; he just didn't know it! When Elijah arrived, he told her to make him a little cake and feed him first, which didn't necessarily go over well with the woman, but she complied. When Elijah's faith touched the little bit of provision she had, they both got a miracle. Her provision never ran out and got her through a drought season, and Elijah got a relaunch into ministry. Obedience plus sacrifice are two powerful spiritual principles that get God's attention and will trigger breakthrough!

God can use anyone to help feed His people. In the story about Elijah in 1 Kings 17, God used ravens to bring him food. If He can use ravens, He can certainly speak to people and impress on their heart what He wants them to do for someone else! On another one of our 'down-to-nothing' days, a young lady from the apartments we lived in came to tell us she would be gone for a few days, and in her hands was a pot roast. She asked us if we would like it and explained that she didn't want it to go to waste while she was away. On another occasion, a different neighbor showed up unexpectedly with a pot full of crawfish, corn and boiled potatoes. God was so good to think of us! We thanked Him for the way He spoke to people and impressed upon them to bring us food. It may not have always been our favorite things, but He didn't let us go hungry. Do you think God can't take care of you? He most certainly can! You do not have to figure out where it is going to come from; you only need to believe that He will be faithful to take care of you.

"Look at the birds of the sky. They do not store food for the winter. They don't plant gardens. They do not sow or reap – and yet, they are always fed because your heavenly Father feeds them. And you are even more precious to Him than a beautiful bird. *If He looks after them, of course He will look after you.*" [2]

---

[2] Matthew 6:26, The Voice

CHAPTER 2

HE KNOWS ME

Learning how to trust God takes time. There were many years when I was a struggling single mom, just doing my best to survive. It wasn't easy trying to figure out how to navigate a relationship with the Lord. It was awkward at first, like any new relationship, and we all have to work through the issue of learning to trust someone we can't see. Many times I wanted to ask, "Is anybody out there?"

The way I learned to understand that He cared for me was through answered prayer. Life as a single mom was tough. It was extremely stressful, especially when there wasn't enough dollars to last through the end of the month. Every month we took the little bit in the coin jar over to the supermarket to cash it in at the Coinstar machine. There was one time my daughter and I went to a Vons grocery store, and when we walked past the Coinstar machine there was absolutely no one around. I glanced down and there was a receipt for cash sticking out of the machine. I kept thinking maybe someone left it and they would come back for it, so I waited for a bit, but no one came to get it. Finally, my daughter said, "Mom, have you ever thought maybe God put that there for you to find? Maybe that's His way of blessing you!" That hadn't occurred to me, but I could tell that no one seemed to be coming back for the cash receipt, so I said, "Thank you, Jesus, for leaving this here," and we used it to buy a few groceries.

I had another "Coinstar miracle" that occurred a different time. It was the end of the month and once again time to empty the coin jar. I didn't have much hope that particular time. We had been dipping into the jar throughout the month just to buy a gallon of milk or put a few dollars in the gas tank. I estimated there was maybe around $10 or $12 dollars in the jar. I prayed that somehow it would be enough to get some groceries, then I poured it into a Ziploc bag and headed for the store. It was around 10:30 at night. I had purposely gone late at night because I was ashamed at how broke we were and I didn't want to face anyone. That sure didn't go as planned! I had no sooner gotten out of the car and started across the parking lot when the bag broke. Coins went everywhere! First one lady, then a couple of other people saw what had happened and started to help me pick up the coins. I kept insisting they didn't have to help and they insisted on helping. So much for trying to remain invisible! I was so embarrassed I felt like I could have just melted into the pavement and disappeared! I had gathered up what seemed to be quite a bit more than what I started with, and finally had the coins back in my purse. I wasn't sure how that happened, but I went to redeem them and lo and behold – it was over $40! I couldn't believe it. Suddenly, my embarrassment turned to relief as I realized that somehow in the midst of the mess God had given me a miracle of multiplication. I marveled at how He had done that right under my nose. He is full of surprises and endless ways of providing for His children! Let me share some other stories of how He provided for me as a single mom.

In one situation, I had been struggling to take care of a fix-it ticket that I had gotten due to a crack in my windshield. I kept putting it off because I didn't have the money, but eventually I had to take care of it. I prayed and asked God to somehow help me pay the bill. It came to a little over $200. As I wrote the check to cover the bill, I wondered how I was going to manage on $200 less that month, especially since I lived paycheck to paycheck and there was never enough to cover all my expenses. That afternoon when I got home, I checked the mail. I was shocked and overjoyed to find an unexpected child support check – in the exact amount of the check I had just written to pay for a new windshield! Coincidence? Not a chance. That was God reassuring me that He knew all about it!

The Lord is faithful. Not because we always live a perfect life, but because we belong to Him. As a new Christian, I began to learn about tithing. One night as I went to bed, I started mentally balancing my checkbook. Suddenly, I realized I had paid bills but forgot to write a check for my tithe. I asked God to forgive me but I felt terrible about it. The next day I walked into work and there was an envelope sitting on my keyboard at my workstation. Inside was a check and a note that said, "The Lord told me you need this much." It wasn't an even amount and it was down to the dollars and cents. I called my bank and there was one check that had not cleared, but I didn't have as much as I thought. The difference between the amount of the check vs. what I had in the bank was one cent! Since God is never wrong, I chalked that one up to bank error. I would have been overdrawn by the exact amount of the check that was in the envelope, but He was helping me cover that check so that I wouldn't be overdrawn. Is that amazing or what? God has people that hear from Him with incredible accuracy! He knows everything about us and He is able to send help when it's needed.

Now this next story is truly interesting! I had answered the phone at the church and was surprised to find a complete stranger asking to speak to me. I listened as this person explained that they had somehow gotten a piece of mail delivered to them. Not once, *but three times* a particular piece of mail was sent to them by mistake. I was truly baffled! What was odd is that they lived across town and there was no reason in the world why that piece of mail should been delivered to them. All they knew is that it had my name on it, and the name of our church. They actually had to call a couple different churches by the same name to see if there was someone by my name that attended there! As they explained the story of repeatedly putting this article of mail back in the outgoing mail, they finally took measures in their own hands to insure that it got to me. The curious letter did indeed arrive a few days later, inside a new envelope. I could see the scribbling on the outside of the envelope and the multiple stamps from the post office trying to redirect the letter to the right address. What was on the inside of the envelope was even more surprising! A $50 money order with my name on it, wrapped inside a simple note that said, "Jesus loves you." The name, address and signature on the money order were completely illegible. I had no idea who had sent it. The $50 was also significant. I had wrestled for quite a while with whether or not I could afford to put more in the weekly offering, and I had just put in my first $50 check that week. The letter had been shuffled around in the mail for over three weeks, but got to me right on time to let me know that God saw my step of faith. After all that, all I could say was thank you. He went to a lot of trouble to make sure I got a very special letter!

Jesus is indeed a good husband. While I was at work one day, unbeknownst to me, a service technician from the electric company was at my house getting ready to turn off my service. I had no clue! I guess I wasn't paying attention, but even if I had, I didn't have the money to pay the bill on time. At the exact time he was there about to disconnect my service, someone from the church I attended drove by to see if I was home. They saw what was happening and very kindly paid the bill for me, which allowed me to avoid the embarrassment and inconvenience of having my service disconnected. Jesus has always shown His faithfulness. I was rescued once again.

But wait – there's more!

There was a time when I had fallen way behind in my bills. I suppose you could say that I pretty much lived that way all the time. I didn't make enough to make ends meet, so I would juggle which bills I could pay from month to month. The stress of it was a lot of pressure to carry, and it brought a lot of bitter emotions to the surface. I remember talking to the Lord one day while I was driving, and I felt the Holy Spirit convicting my heart to forgive my ex-husband. I blamed him for the difficulties of raising a child alone and without enough money to do it better. He had dodged his obligations repeatedly while I struggled to pay bills, raise a daughter on my own and put food on the table. I was mad and discouraged at the fact that life was so hard, and at that moment I really didn't appreciate God getting in my business! Nevertheless, I felt the Lord nudging me to forgive him. I had this feeling that God wanted to bless me but couldn't until I did my part. I finally did what He asked. I told the Lord I forgave him for the pain and disappointment he had caused me and my daughter. At first, it was really hard to want to pray, but as I continued I found that I actually meant what I was praying. It just wasn't worth it to carry all that anger around with me. I wanted to be free. All of a sudden, my heart was full of peace. The situation hadn't changed, but I had. I felt like God had His hand over my heart. He kept me in perfect peace, even though two whole weeks passed and nothing changed. Then one day someone from church came to me and said, "How much do you need to pay your bills?" Bring them to me. That was difficult. I felt so ashamed that I couldn't pay them. This person looked them over and told me that they were going to help me. I had over $700 in unpaid bills and the whole stack got paid! Then I was blessed with money for food. I was so humbled by God's goodness I started to say, "Oh no, it's too much, it's too much." I was literally overwhelmed with the goodness of God! How's that for a blessing?

Little by little, it finally began to dawn on me that God really knew me. His uncanny ways of showing up in the nick of time to take care of my needs was proof! He wasn't someone that stood off in the distance, unconcerned about my welfare. No, my Father got involved in my life and took good care of me. It really is a thought that inspires wonder and amazement! Friend, you have a heavenly father that loves you! My Father showed me time after time that He took note of the details of my life. He reached out to show me in some very practical ways that He cared about me. God wants to personalize our relationship with Him, because when we know Him, we will learn to trust Him. When we learn to trust Him, our faith grows immensely.

"O Eternal One, You have explored my heart and know exactly who I am. You even know the small details, like when I take a seat and when I stand up again. Even when I am far away, You know what I am thinking. You observe my wanderings and my sleeping, my waking and my dreaming; and You know everything I do in more detail that even I know. You know what I'm going to say long before I say it. It is true, Eternal One, that You know everything and everyone. You have surrounded me on every side, behind me and before me, and You have placed Your hand gently on my shoulder. It is the most amazing feeling to know how deeply You know me, inside and out; the realization of it is so great I cannot comprehend it."[3]

---

[3] Psalm 139:1-6, The Voice

CHAPTER 3
BEYOND OUR UNDERSTANDING

We have to get used to the idea that God works in ways we won't understand. I didn't understand why He waited until we had absolutely nothing at all to work with before He would release His help. God's process of preparation can seem backwards and frustrating, but it's His way of proving to us that nothing is impossible when we put our faith in Him! Time and time again He put us in miracle needing situations so that we would exercise our faith and learn to stand on His word.

After a period of time in Florida, we thought a door of opportunity was opening in a new location. We had traveled back and forth for several months on a personal recommendation from our pastor, who had recommended us to a potential employer at another church. It took us three months to realize that we had put our trust in the wrong person. It wasn't God opening a door. God didn't send us there; man did, which is why nothing came together as we had hoped. We learned that sometimes, what seemed like God can just be someone else's good intentions. We kept waiting for a confirming word on the job and interview process, but God wasn't speaking to the person making decisions because He hadn't sent us there! We felt foolish, frustrated and by the time we figured it out, we had exhausted all our finances. Our bank account literally said $0.00. That was the precise moment my husband announced he was going to start a flooring business. I looked at him like he was crazy! *"When exactly did you do that?"* I asked. "Oh, about 15 or 20 years ago," was his reply. *What???* During all the years I had known him I had not known he had any experience with flooring. My mind was racing with wild thoughts. Why was this new information? Could he still do what he did before? Was he out of his mind? I thought he had totally lost it! A wave of uncontrollable fear hit me like a ton of bricks. We had a new baby, no money and my husband was actually entertaining the idea of starting a business with no money. That was either total craziness or a big leap of faith. My mind being where it was that day decided crazy sounded like the more likely option. A horrible sense of dread settled over me and it was really hard to shake. Things felt like they were getting worse by the minute!

Thankfully, God proved me wrong. There is an old proverb that says, "Necessity is the mother of invention." Another quote by play writer George Chapman states, "The great mother of all productions is **grave necessity**." We have found this to be true!

It is important to learn to look at discomfort and frustration as opportunities for change. Unmet needs are indicators to start looking for answers outside the box. If the answers you need are not inside the box, start looking for what is outside the box. 'Boxes' represent everything inside your comfort zone. Getting outside your box requires confronting fear and insecurities about ourselves. Why are we insecure about trying new things? Are our fears tied to some situation or disappointment from the past? Inside the box is what we know, but change requires doing new things in unfamiliar places. You will never find the answers you need if the place where you're planted is not the place God has designed for you to prosper and grow.

Don't make your God too small! People limit what God can do when they insist on staying within the confines of their comfort zone. He longs to take us on an adventure! He longs to hear his children ask Him to do things so big that they can't possibly do it in their own strength. He puts us in awkward, uncomfortable, impossible situations so that we have to ask Him to do what we cannot. The fear of looking foolish to others can keep us from taking risks. If pride and staying within the confines of our comfort zone are more important than letting God get the glory for doing something great in our life, we will never fulfill our potential. This is where faith is activated, and faith is the commodity of the kingdom. It's the only real currency we will ever need to operate in God's economy.

Difficult situations are the opportunity we need to inspire

creative solutions. Unless we are pressed to do something different, we won't look for a new solution. Miracles take place when people are stuck between a rock and a hard place. Uncomfortable situations can be God's gift to birth inspiration and a display of His glory!

Once again, Jesus rode in to rescue us. It wasn't easy building a business from scratch, and even more difficult when you have nothing to work with, but you know what? God did it. If He did it for us, He can help you, too! Every time God did something in our life, it wasn't when we had enough or things were going smoothly. It was when we had nothing to work with that God moved – because that is when desperation pulled something out of the invisible realm. God loves to create new things out of nothing just to prove ALL THINGS ARE POSSIBLE WITH HIM!

We went back to the pastor and told him what was going on, and asked him if he knew of anyone that might be able to help us with some connections. It was a fairly sizable church and we thought perhaps he could refer us to someone that might be able to help. The person we were referred to just happened to walk across the church parking lot as we walked to our car. He suggested a few things that were helpful and then he referred us to someone else. That sort of thing happened several times. Each new person would give Norm advice on what steps to take. Those things led to work, a business license and other important connections. Little by little, the business started to grow. God blessed Norm with work and he never had to advertise. Word of mouth referrals kept him busy. Until, of course, God let us know He had other plans.

A few years later – and quite unexpectedly - God told us to surrender the business. He also told us to commit to the change. We didn't understand why He would say that because the business was actually doing quite well. Once again, we found God doing things that were completely unpredictable. After all, He helped us build the business from scratch. Why would He tell us to surrender it? It didn't make sense to us, but we figured He had to have a purpose that we hadn't yet figured out, and something better for the future.

We didn't know what to expect, but we were obedient to follow His leading. As soon as we told the Lord we would honor His request, it was as if work supernaturally dried up. No matter what Norm did to look for work, it was like trying to pry doors open. He went around town putting in resumes, but nothing came of it. We could not understand why on earth God would do something so extreme that led us into deep poverty and need. Suddenly, I didn't like God's idea of whatever that 'something better' might be; I wanted my life back! That ship had sailed and we were in deep water. There was no turning back, and we were way out of our comfort zone! We also knew He was looking for sacrifice. He was looking for people that were sold out to Him no matter what, and we wanted to be the people that said yes to His plan, but I'll admit that was the hardest test we've ever walked through.

That step of faith allowed us to go through another very deep valley of disappointment. We have at times analyzed and re-analyzed everything that unfolded and what we heard from God. I'm not sure if we made some serious errors in our understanding back then or not, but there was simply no mistaking the chain of events that took place. None of those things would have occurred if it hadn't been for honoring what we felt we heard from God. He tested us to see if we would sacrifice everything for the sake of the kingdom. If you've read a couple of our other books then you may be familiar with this story.

Once again we got down to nothing, only that time God didn't show up with the answer, at least not the way we had come to expect. His ways are so different than ours! What we didn't understand at the time was the fact that He wanted us to become the answer for others. Each one of us has been created as an answer to someone else's prayers! We ended up sowing a little pan of tuna casserole into a few homeless people, hoping God would take that seed offering and do something with it. He did!

Giving away what we needed most – food – set off a domino effect that released supernatural activity in our lives. These were things we never could have anticipated! Ladies from our home group wanted to get involved and they helped birth a ministry to the homeless, where we ended up feeding $75-100 people every week. It rained a lot in Florida, so just about every week we commanded the clouds to hold their rain until we were done ministering to people, and those clouds obeyed! With the exception of once or twice, those clouds obeyed! That was just one of many miracles. Every Tuesday we would be out in Corrine Jones Park in Pensacola, and we saw God answer many prayers of the homeless.

God made a lot of divine connections through that park ministry. He used a little pan of tuna casserole and 12 Pillsbury biscuits to launch a ministry in the streets of Pensacola. He also opened the doors to favor with the city, which allowed us to hold a couple of multi-church, city-wide events. Believe me, God can use the little that we have to do great things! One of the miraculous things He provided during that time was the paperwork for a non-profit corporation, known as a 501C3. The forms from the city required the identification number from a 501C3, but we didn't know that until we were already committed to the evangelistic events. At the time, we didn't have a non-profit. We thought we would have to pull the plug on the plans to do the outreach. Then we got a phone call.

On the phone was a man we went to church with, and he had heard God was doing some interesting things with ministry to those outside the church. Mark told us that he had the corporate paperwork for a non-profit called His Hands Outreach but God had never done anything with it. It was designed for Christians in transition that needed provision and answers to practical needs until they established stability. He was about ready to just let the corporation dissolve, then he heard God tell him to bless us with the corporate paperwork. This man had done everything to lay the foundation for the corporation believing that one day God would do something to use it for a greater purpose, but it just sat there for 4 years. Just when time was running out and it was about to dissolve, God decided to use it to help us. We were able to complete the forms for the city so that we could hold the outreach. Isn't it amazing how He puts things together? Our Father knows exactly what we need at any given moment and He knows who to speak to so that we can continue to carry out kingdom plans and purposes!

God led people from the community out to help in the park. It always amazed me how powerfully God used the little bit we were doing to touch people's hearts. It made us realize the hunger level in the body of Christ. Some people wanted to observe what we were doing, and others went there to receive prayer. Many people felt inspired to get involved and they wanted to volunteer. One of the wonderful things that happened was the people from the local crack house across the street came over and asked for deliverance. God brought a number of women who wanted deliverance from their involvement in witchcraft. A lot of great things happened in that park, but we were still struggling to survive because God had told us to surrender the business. It wasn't that Norm didn't look for work, but God was doing a very deep work in our hearts, and the struggle that we went through seemed to be a part of His plan. We had to live the reality that the homeless people experienced; not knowing where our next meal would come from, not having work and sometimes not having gas in the car to provide transportation. It was rough. That may not fit with a lot of people's theology, but that's what God did with us. Our hearts were torn with a level of compassion that we hadn't known before. We understood the fear and frustration of doing everything we knew how to do, yet restoration seemed out of reach. All we could do was survive one day at a time and keep on praying.

If it hadn't been for those very difficult times, I am not sure we would have learned as much as we did. Not just about God, but about ourselves and others. There are some things a person just doesn't learn until they have walked in someone else's shoes. Many people were quick to judge and offer their religious opinions. The way God was working in our lives didn't fit within the confines of their perception. To be honest, a lot didn't fit with our understanding, either. He may not work that way in everyone's life, but He was doing something unique in ours. All we could do was go along for the ride. During that time we had to learn how to trust God all over again, because He was using others to help support us. It taught us dependence on Him, and it also taught us humility. Part of the reason we went through those things was to remove any desire whatsoever to judge other people's circumstances.

It can be so easy to pass judgement on others without really knowing why they are going through certain things or what God is doing to perfect their love for Him. Religious pride can make a person feel superior or justified for those judgments, but eventually those judgments we make against others becomes the groundwork for our own judgment.[4] The things we despise in others becomes something that is exposed in us. It may be a different season, but the word of God remains true. Judgements and criticisms create pain and offense. God, in His mercy, teaches us not to judge others by allowing us to experience what others have gone through. He has a way of taking us through things that work to produce genuine repentance and humility. Experience can make a permanent heart change better than any sermon. Although it's been said, "It is more blessed to give than receive," it's important to understand what it feels like when you're in a humble place and dependent upon the kindness of others. We needed to know how to bless others and show compassion without causing them to lose their sense of dignity. God teaches every one of His children this lesson.

It was a humbling blow to lose our home. We felt devastated and no matter how well we tried to get through it, it was a disappointment so deep that it affected us for a long time afterwards. God was still faithful to provide shelter, but it was no longer a home of our own. We felt betrayed because we didn't understand all that God was doing. At the time, we had no idea that God was preparing to uproot us again and send us back to California. That thought hadn't occurred to us, and we weren't asking the right questions. It

---

[4] Matthew 7:1,2

took a long time to figure out that's why nothing was coming together to provide for us there, but I'll tell you that part of the story in another chapter!

We went through a long season of being dependent on the kindness of others and trusting God through that time of transition. A friend let us stay with her for a month. Then, on the last day - when we had no idea where we were to go next - the phone rang. It was a woman that we had been involved with in the park ministry. She had a house on the beach and offered to let us stay there for a couple of weeks. We gratefully accepted. When our time there was nearly over, again we found ourselves in that place of tension, not knowing what came next. We got another phone call. This time it was someone we didn't know personally, but wanted to help us out. One of their family members had a condo on a different beach and they offered to let us stay there for a couple of weeks.

One day a woman came to the park looking for us. She had her checkbook in hand and told us that God told her to drive out there and give us a check for $33.30. I asked her what was the significance of the odd amount. She said it was because God gave her Jeremiah 33:3 as a scripture verse to encourage us. No matter how difficult the circumstances got, He made sure to let us know that He was there in the midst of the battle. He never left us, and He won't leave you, either.

"This is my last gift to you, this example of a way of life: a life of hard work, a life of helping the weak, a life that echoes every day those words of Jesus our King, who said, "It is more blessed to give than receive."[5]

---

[5] Acts 20:35, The VOICE

CHAPTER 4
JUST ENOUGH

When nothing comes together no matter how much you're trying to make something work, it is often an indicator that God is leading in another direction. It took us quite a while to figure out that's what He was doing, but we knew the significance of doors closing. We struggled to make it through one of the most difficult times in our life, and it was painfully obvious that we weren't anywhere near the end of that season. We were stuck in a holding pattern but we didn't know why, until we received a call that Norm's brother was dying of pancreatic cancer.

We wanted to see him, but Norm's brother lived in Canada, and we did not have the finances or the other things necessary to make the trip. It was right after Christmas, and winter in Canada was severe. Nevertheless, we believed God wanted us to go, so we began to pray about how we might make the trip. We told the Lord that if

He wanted us to go to Canada, He would have to provide winter clothes and suitcases for our family. We also needed repairs to our van that were quite costly. Every door to employment had closed, and we had been renting a motor home for a few hundred dollars a month. Then the owner told us he needed it back because he was taking a trip. We had no idea what to do next, two little ones under the age of 4, and our pets. We seemed to live in a constant state of transition and readiness to move when God pulled up the stakes at one place and directed us somewhere else. He had always been faithful to provide, but it was very meager rations. For the longest time it just seemed like punishment. I was so angry with God!

It really was only after that season was over that I could look back and reflect how God had perfect timing in everything He did to provide for us. The constant desperation of our circumstances forced us to grow in ways we wouldn't have chosen for ourselves. Our faith was stretched to the breaking point over and over and over, but that is what caused us to expect more from God. It also caused us to put a demand on the anointing and not take no for an answer! Like Abraham of old, we learned to 'call those things that did not exist as though they did,' and demanded they show up. We learned how to pray in every bit of provision. There were times when we would find bags of groceries left anonymously on the front step. One time I went to shut off the outside light and there was a basket of fruit sitting by the door. There was a card inside with words of encouragement and a couple hundred dollars in cash. At other times, a friend here or a friend there would let us know that God had put it into their hearts to bless us with something to help meet our needs. God showed His loving care for us many times. It definitely stretched our faith, and to be quite honest, I hated every minute of it! I had wrestled with my perspective of God for many years, and I tended to see Him more in the light of being difficult to please and quick to punish, so it took me a long, long time to realize that was not what He was doing. Our faith doesn't grow in the easy times. It grows in the hard times. Faith grows through adversity, and God really wanted me to understand that I had misjudged Him, so He kept giving me opportunities to trust Him and see how faithful He was to take care of us. I didn't realize that's what He was up to! It was a frightening time, not knowing how we were going to take care of our family, but God was working out our trust issues and trying to show us that He was able to provide for us even in the most difficult circumstances.

There is something that happens when you go through the same type of faith-stretching exercises over and over again. You face your fears. You also learn that God is faithful and He will come through for you. Eventually I realized that even though I hated the process, I knew God would keep feeding us and taking care of us. His track record proved it. We were living the reality of what the Israelites dealt with being led through the wilderness. Every bit of provision was meager but sufficient. He always waited until I was on the edge of panic, but His purpose through it all was to strengthen our faith.

There was one time when I had no more diapers for my son, and I was very upset about it. We had a newborn and no diapers. That was a problem! I turned the house upside down. I dug through purses, diaper bags and tore the car apart looking for a diaper, but there were none anywhere. I started declaring, "God, enough is enough! You said you are my provider. You said You are my Shepherd and I will not lack. In Jesus name I will not lack diapers, and I insist they show up right now!" Well, do you know what happened? About an hour later I needed to change my son, but I knew that there were no more diapers. For some reason, I went to the basket anyway, and there it was – *one* diaper! It had not been there earlier. I knew for a fact it had not been there! I said, "Lord, thank you for the diaper, but couldn't you have provided more?" And He said, "How many does your son need right now?" God has a sense of humor, even if we don't always appreciate it! A little while later we received a check and we were able to buy a package of diapers. Once again God got us over the rough spot.

God also brought in everything that was needed for the trip to Canada to go visit Norm's brother. Almost as soon as I had finished praying, I got a call from a friend that had winter gear, clothing and suitcases. I marked those off my list. Then someone else called and said they would pay for the repairs on the van. That was $1200.00! We knew we were supposed to make the trip because God was answering, but we had very little cash. We only had about $600, and that was barely enough to get one way. We had no money to get very far in any direction, and somehow we had to get back to Florida to get our things out of storage. However, there were no longer open doors for us, so we could only move in the direction God was leading us. We had no idea where we would end up, but we proceeded to make plans for the trip.

At this point, we were facing our fears on a daily basis, but we believed that somehow God would show us what to do. As we left Florida and crossed into Alabama, a semi-truck with the words "Jehovah Jireh" passed us and led the way. It gave us great comfort to see those words! Jehovah Jireh means Yahweh (God) will provide. About an hour later, a friend of someone we knew but had never met, called us and offered to pay for our hotel that night. God's miracle provision kicked in again!

A couple days later my daughter, who was 4 at the time, came to me and said, "Mommy, do you know that God is going to give us money?" I was tired, discouraged and I felt very beat down. It had been a long bumpy journey of meager rations and the stress of constantly living in survival mode had taken its toll. I was not really in the mood for entertaining false hope. I thought she was just trying to make me feel better. I should have learned to trust God by then, but I still struggled because of all the lies in my belief system and the instability of what we had been going through. We were in the middle of the Midwest, which at the time felt a lot like being lost at sea. Shocked and a bit sarcastically I shot back, "Oh really? When did He say that?" Without missing a beat, my daughter matter-of-factly said, "Just now, when I was in the kitchen." My mouth dropped open in wonder. When I was too overwhelmed to hear from God, He spoke through my little one. Their hearts are so pure! She heard correctly too, because at every stop on the way people put money in our hands or paid for a hotel. It was always just enough to get to the next place. He even influenced people that didn't know Him! I have learned to listen when my kids feel they've heard something from the Lord. He may not always speak to us. He may put the answers or encouragement we need in someone else. It's our job to make sure we're listening!

During the time we had been traveling, we somehow managed to get our taxes done and we received a tax refund check into our account. After our trip to Canada, the refund check allowed us to travel back to Florida to retrieve our belongings out of storage. During the trip, Norm had decided that if we were going to be broke, we could just as easily be broke in California but at least we would be closer to our adult children. We missed them terribly and decided that we needed to follow our heart. Before we left, we asked some friends at a local church to pray for us. Once again we had to make the trip by faith. God had given me a dream that I felt was confirmation we should go back to California, and that was about the only thing we had to go on! The church not only prayed for us, they *sent* us. They took an offering that helped us get back to California. God came through – but once again it was just barely enough to meet the need. We were following God in blind faith, not knowing what we were doing or where we would end up.

"Remember how the Eternal, your True God, led you through the wilderness these past 40 years. He did this to humble you, to test you, to uncover your motivations, to see if You would obey His commands. He humbled you by making you hungry when there was no food in the desert. Then He fed you with manna, a food you and your ancestors had never heard of. He did this because He wanted you to understand that what makes you truly alive is not the bread you eat but following every word that comes from the mouth of the Eternal One." [6]

---

[6] Deut. 8:1-4, The VOICE

CHAPTER 5
DIVINE CONNECTIONS

If it hadn't been for the trip to Canada and back to Florida that we had just made, we never would have had the faith to make the trip to California. God had been preparing our hearts for another radical step of faith, even though we didn't know that was what would eventually take place.

The knowledge that God had supernaturally provided for that trip caused our faith to be at an all-time high. We didn't make the trip to say goodbye to Norm's brother; we went believing for a miracle. There was healing and restoration that took place and Norm's brother got a miracle in his body that allowed him to live an extra couple of years.

Making the trip back to California wasn't necessarily the difficult part. We had enough to get us one way. What we didn't have was work or a place to live. We stayed with our oldest son for a couple of weeks, then moved to a hotel. Our funds were dangerously low, and we decided to go to a "Miracle Monday" prayer night at one of the local churches. It was in the presence of God that Norm had a vision of us wearing T-shirts with the words, "Praying for Our City" and going on a prayer walk. We were there seeking God for answers for practical needs and He suggested a prayer walk instead! God really does work in mysterious ways. We couldn't possibly fathom how He would bring them to pass! That is why it is so important not to try to figure things out in our own strength but to get in the presence of God where we can receive thoughts from the Holy Spirit.

God makes things happen when we choose to be obedient to what He reveals, even though it may not make sense in the natural. We began to go on prayer walks around different parts of the county. From the coastal areas to the Mexican border and back, we simply prayed for our city and the needs of others we met along the way. A local Baptist pastor had met Norm at a prayer meeting several weeks before and asked us to take him and some of his elders on a prayer walk around their neighborhood in Vista. They were not familiar with prayer walks and wanted to learn more. We passed a park that was known for gang activity and drug dealing, and stopped to pray. There was a young man that saw we were praying and he started to scream obscenities at us and demand that we stop praying. I walked forward to approach him and he cussed us out even more! I said, "Holy Spirit, go get him!" He took off running! Then another unusual thing happened. A man driving by suddenly did a U-turn and screeched to a halt next to us, and he asked what we were doing. When we told him we were praying, this man asked if he could join us! He went on to tell us that he had been one of the drug dealers and gang members that had frequented the park but God saved him. He said he went back to the park to witness to others in hopes that they, too, would get saved. He insisted we meet his pastor and asked us to come to church with him, so we did. When the pastor heard our story he said, "You've got to meet *my* pastor!" A few days later we met his pastor, whose name was David. Norm was surprised to walk in and meet a man he had known about 15 years earlier. Pastor David also remembered Norm. When he heard our story, he was very touched. He also told us we were probably a little bit crazy to haul our family all over like we did having no money and no plan! It was so evident that God had made these connections for us, using a very unconventional strategy of taking us on a prayer walk. We knew He had orchestrated the meetings, but we didn't know how significant those relationships would become until later.

During this time, the Baptist pastor we had met a few weeks earlier had called and asked if we would house sit while they were away on vacation. They would be gone several weeks. That helped solve another housing problem for a few weeks. On the day they were scheduled to come home, we were cleaning the place and once again packing all our belongings into our van. My heart was so heavy. We had no idea where we would stay that night. Out of desperation, I had placed an ad on Craigslist which basically said ministry family willing to work off rent in exchange for housing. I really didn't expect it to work. It was a horrible feeling to have all our stuff in the van, including our cat and our kids, who were 4 and 18 months at the time. I could barely hold myself together. It was 4:00 in the afternoon and we had run out of options. All we could do was pray. Suddenly, Norm's phone rang and it was a woman who lived in the Midwest. She had seen our ad on Craigslist. This woman was a minister in another state but she also owned a home in San Diego. Although she had never met us, she decided to take a chance and allow us the opportunity to rent her home. We met her brother at the house and he gave us the keys. We could hardly believe it. Talk about a divine connection!

It would have been great had that been the end of the story, but Norm still did not have work coming in, and that posed a huge problem trying to pay rent. We were able to feed ourselves off of love offerings from others but it wasn't enough to pay bills. We stayed in the house a month, but then had to surrender the house. This was the third house that we lost and I was really, really angry with God. Once again, a major wave of disappointment and discouragement left us feeling completely overwhelmed. Even in the midst of that, God continued to provide miraculously. We found a storage place that was running a special. They offered the first 30 days for free and threw in a free tank of gas as well, so we were able to put our belongings in storage for free.

On the day we had to move, the pastor from the church came to help us along with a couple of other men. All day long I heard the Lord say, "Will you trust me?" I was so mad! I hadn't been able to feed my kids at all that day and I was losing it. We literally did not have one dollar to our name. I said, "NO! I will not trust You. I trusted You and look what happened. I don't want to talk to You!" How's that for being real with God? I was so miserable and discouraged I didn't know what to do with myself. What I could not understand during that time is that I was truly looking at the situation from the wrong perspective. I was accusing God of not taking care of us, but it never occurred to me that there was a specific reason why things were happening in that way. Pastor David had called Norm and invited us to come stay with him. We really didn't want to impose but we were stuck and had run out of options. When there is only one door open, you have to go towards that door! Going to stay with people we didn't know left us feeling terribly awkward, humbled and ashamed that we were in that situation. Pastor David's family overwhelmed us with their kind, gracious attitude. What we didn't know is that God had lined up a blessing, and if we hadn't been staying in his house we would have missed it!

Pastor David gave us the keys to his truck, his credit card, and told us to go get whatever we needed. I was stunned. Who did that? I had never encountered that kind of unconditional love and generosity. We felt humbled by the kindness this family showed us. The relationship was immediate love and friendship. Divine connections feel like you've known someone far longer than you have in reality. We had resisted because we didn't want to be an imposition, but God had ways for us to mutually bless one another. It was during our stay there that David went to meet a friend one day for breakfast. His friend, John, wanted to share a testimony with him about how God had gotten him out of retirement to give him a property management business! When David came back from his meeting he said, "Hey, I told my friend about you and your crazy story, and he says he knows you!" As it turned out, the man remembered Norm's brother from Bible College 30 years earlier and remembered Norm, too. It just so happened that God used John to give Norm work on a couple of his properties. Shortly after that divine connection, John gave us the keys to move in to a vacant apartment. No down payment, no credit check, just a kind word from an old friend and a gentle nudge from the Holy Spirit. As it happened, the day we needed to move into the new apartment was the very last day of the 30 day special on the storage space, and we ended up not having to pay one dime. God had lined everything up that was needed! It had been close to a year of constant moving and living out of suitcases. I told the Lord that if He didn't give us rest, I was going to have a nervous breakdown. Thankfully, the Lord allowed us to settle down for several years in the same place.

One of the amazing things about that story is that God had to get John out of retirement and give him someone else's business before John had the ability to be a blessing to us. Do you see how He is always at work, taking care of the details? God has specific places where we will encounter the people He has lined up bless us. Sometimes we cannot connect with the blessings because we're not in the right place. That is why it is very important to let Him lead us!

During this time we had been invited to several churches to come share our testimony. We were surprised that people kept telling our story and wanted to meet the couple who were crazy enough to follow God without a roadmap or a plan. On one occasion, I had met a total stranger and somehow we had gotten to talking, sharing a little bit about ourselves. All of a sudden her eyes lit up and she said, "You're that couple! I just heard our pastor share your testimony at church a couple weeks ago, and now I'm sitting here talking to you!" It was another odd moment that just made me scratch my head in wonder. Our story seemed to get people's attention, and people kept re-telling it to others.

I learned something through that. Sometimes the testimonies that you don't want people to know are the ones they need to hear. From our perspective, all we could relate to was the embarrassment of not being able to provide for our family. The feeling of humiliation kept us locked up behind walls of fear, not wanting to subject ourselves to more feelings of dishonor, but what other people took away from our stories was a sense of hope for their own struggles. The testimonies of His constant care and provision for our family helped others recognize God's love and commitment to take care of His children was genuine, and they felt comforted to know that He would take care of them, too.

Many people also recognized there was an anointing to walk in the supernatural, and they lined up to receive prayer. They realized by all our crazy testimonies that God was with us, and it elevated their faith to believe God would do something in their own difficult problems. When you walk with God in the kind of situations we had faced, it really does do something to your faith. It forces it to come alive! The only thing that tells us something is impossible is our own mind. We had to learn to stop looking at all the impossibilities and focus on God's promises. He had a good track record. Although we didn't always like His process, He was always faithful. The stories you're reading in this book are not rare. God works in miraculous ways for people all the time. We were in a recent church service and the pastor asked a question of the congregation. "If you can remember a time when God came through for you," he said, "Would you please stand up?" Every single person in the church stood up. That should tell you something about God's faithfulness to His children!

I must point out that there were many times on our journey that we struggled with bad attitudes, discouragement, self-pity, and doubt. We had times of feeling completely disconnected from the body of Christ. We struggled with a lack of strength and various other frustrations, but sometimes the way we grow with God is to be left alone with Him. It's important to be transparent on this issue. A religious attitude will tell you that you always have to be connected to a local church, but sometimes God works differently in people's lives. Sometimes people go through seasons of being out of church in order to take off the religious filters and break off condemnation and false guilt. When people are going through an extended period of stress and difficulty, they are also hurting from internal emotional pain associated with the traumatic events of their lives. It is nearly impossible to have an accurate understanding of God's heart when we process information through a filter of brokenness. That filter alters our perception, twists truth, and causes us to misunderstand the intent of God's heart. The filter creates more pain and misunderstanding, which causes people to also accuse God of being hard to please, harsh and someone that can't be trusted. Sometimes people feel condemnation because they don't know what to do to help get their life back on track, but those things serve to further separate people from God. They may feel their failures or their lack of understanding are signs of being rejected by God. Those were all issues of my life that caused an internal war in my soul, but my feelings did not represent truth.

God's love is incredibly longsuffering. His hand is always outstretched to us, beckoning us to draw closer so that we can understand His heart. When we truly understand Him, His perfect love for us will cast out our fears.

I remember a day when I had gone to apply for government assistance. I definitely had not arrived at that 'perfect love casting out all fear" stage, not by a long shot. I had been holding out for God to intervene in our circumstances, but I was at my wit's end. Another family I knew received food stamps and they received quite a bit for assistance, so I decided to apply for help. I felt like I was being disloyal to God, but I gathered all the paperwork, drove down to the Social Services office, and waited in line for hours only to be told that THAT DAY they had changed some of their qualifying criteria. I would have had to come back with my husband and start the process all over again. I was so discouraged that I left and decided it wasn't worth the trouble. Once I got in the car, all my anger and frustration erupted. I had been hanging on to the end of my rope and it just snapped. Have you ever tried praying and all that comes out is yelling? I shouted, "God, I don't get you! I have done everything I know how to walk right with you. I have repented, over and over for as much as I know to do. The government will give people more money to live on than you are giving us! Is the government supposed to be my God or are You my God? I am ashamed of you right now! It hurts to say that, but Lord I am so mad at you! What we are living is a lie. Is your word truth or not? Because I see your promises and your people were always supposed to be better off than the other nations around them. I'm asking you to rebuke the enemy, and with all due respect, either tell me where we are in sin and we will repent, or turn our finances back on!"

I asked God to forgive me for getting in His face and being disrespectful, but I just didn't understand what we were dealing with or why it was necessary for us to keep struggling to feed our family. The drive home took about 15 minutes, and by the time I got home, my husband had received a call for work and also to pick up a check. It just goes to show that many times the pressure is the greatest right before a breakthrough! We will at times reach that breaking point where we just can't take one more moment of distress, but God hears every prayer and every cry for help. He will come through!

Is anger a sin? Is it wrong to yell at the Creator of the Universe? Yes, I blew it many times! Is it unbelief not to trust God? Is fear a sin? Yes. The Bible tells us that whatever is not in faith is unbelief, and unbelief is sin. Fear is failure to trust God, and we were both full of fear. Sure, we were guilty of missing the mark. Probably every day, too. That's why we're so grateful for the blood of Jesus!

I met one pastor who said to me, "Although it is great to hear that God provided for you, I have to ask, what was really going on in your lives? Did God have to make you homeless just to prove a point?" He proceeded to tell me that he had been a Christian a long time, and God never had to force him into homelessness to get his attention. In his words, "Well the fault doesn't lie with God, so it has to be with you. Couldn't He just have told you what He wanted you to understand?" I felt the heat rising in my face and the flush of embarrassment at his impolite remarks. I was stunned at his insensitivity, but it wasn't the first time we endured the skeptical looks of people that believed we either missed God somewhere along the line or thought we were struggling because God was punishing us. We endured the judgmental attitudes of those who had not walked through what we did, and their insinuations that we must have been too stubborn to 'learn our lesson' any other way.

It was at that precise moment, face-to-face with a sanctimonious, religious attitude, that I realized the path God had taken us through really was necessary. It was necessary because we had come out of a religious, legalistic church that viewed God as a punishing God instead of a gracious Father. Religion always pulls people back under condemnation and the implications of failure. Religion shames people and causes pain and offense because it bases everything on performance. Religion will tell you that if something is going wrong in your life then somewhere you failed to measure up. It makes everything about our own works instead of what Jesus has done for us. *Of course* we fall short – everyday! *Of course* we experience failure, defeat and setbacks; we're human! But, God took care of our sin issue once and for all. Jesus paid the ultimate price for our failures. He took our sin upon Himself and shed His blood in order to pay our debt. His sacrifice allows all who will receive Him a future free from shame and the fear of separation from our heavenly Father.

There were many times we didn't have our feelings all neatly packaged into some politically correct response. It wasn't easy trusting God in those circumstances. We're human. People tend to want to know where they're going, what they're doing, and what to expect. Parents tend to want to know where their babies are going to lay their heads at night. We want to know we have enough diapers, formula and necessities to take care of our kids. We don't *want* to have to pray those things in! Most of us would really be happy knowing we had a roof over our heads and enough food to feed our family. When stress goes up, saintly responses tend to fly out the window. I tell you all this so you know that there were times when we acted completely human.

But, to imply that we weren't seeking God and living 'disconnected' from Him due to willful disobedience, that just reeked of a self-satisfied, holier-than-thou attitude. We lived in a constant state of repentance! We had never renounced so many things in our lives! We did not want anything hindering our prayers so we lived in a continuous state of prayer and seeking God – and He answered time and time again. We were more connected to Him than probably at any other time in our personal history.

Somehow, it was that arrogant question that clinched it in my mind as to all the reasons why the journey *was* necessary. Up until that moment, I really didn't have an answer, and that had been a source of my anger towards God. Suddenly, I understood why God took us through all those things. God couldn't just tell us what He wanted us to understand because we wouldn't have gotten it. We didn't ever want to inflict pain on someone else from religious judgments because we knew how it felt to be judged and criticized. We had to live it so that we would understand the fears, the insecurity, the anger, hurt and resentment that others feel. We needed to understand the feelings of hopelessness, despair and utter helplessness of situations beyond our control. He was birthing a new level of compassion, free from self-righteous judgments. Self-righteousness comes from feeling superior towards others, and it comes from not having personally experienced what others have gone through. It's easy to judge someone else's life when you have no personal experience with the same type of situation. We also needed to understand the hesitancy of people trying to figure out whether or not they could trust God for themselves. There are many people in the world today whose lives have been shattered and they're asking the questions, "Why did this have to happen?" "Can I trust God?" and "How do I start over?" "Does God really care about me?"

Don't get caught up in needing all the answers because that will make you crazy! Sometimes the answers only come when you look back at what you learned from the journey, and other times we may never know this side of heaven. I can look back now, see all the divine connections and how God used each person to help get us through to the next part of our destination. I also know that a lot of the time it wasn't about us, but about people on the way, and the fact that God wanted us to minister to others. We came to realize that sometimes the reason we seemed to be momentarily stuck is because we were the divine connection someone else had been praying for! Even in the midst of our pain and difficulties, we can be a source of comfort, hope and encouragement to others. Many times we found ourselves waiting for a specific encounter before He would get us moving again. God wasn't withholding blessings just to punish us, but thinking about others, too. We hadn't reached our final destination. If He had provided permanent housing or work, we would have settled in that place, but God was still leading us to a new and unfamiliar location where greater blessings would unfold.

I hope that our story reassures others that God does indeed care about all of us. People need a tour guide for their own journey. None of us wants a journey that has been full of pain, but that is just part of life. In this life there will be troubles and difficulty, but we have a Lord and Savior that stands with us through them all. He doesn't leave us alone. God chooses our testimonies for us. He wanted Norm and I to have a testimony that comforted others with the knowledge that we, too, have been in difficult places. We've endured loss, disappointments and we've been without a place to call home. There are a lot of people who in a mere moment have lost homes, businesses, relationships and the security of their jobs. It's the kind of devastation that can leave families teetering on the edge of financial ruin, and many people don't know how to bear up under the strain. We understand the hurt because we've had to live it, but we also know our God is a God that restores better than before!

God needs a people that can minister to others without a sense of self-righteousness or judgment. Bad things happen to people in this life, and many of them due to no fault of their own. I have heard pastors and other ministers tell people, "If you are obedient and pay your tithes and offerings, you'll never suffer lack." We had a pastor once that said he had never suffered lack.. He boasted that he had always been able to pay his bills and seemed unfamiliar with hardship. He praised the benefits of tithing, yet we were sitting in his congregation, still paying tithes and being as dutiful as we knew how, in the midst of losing everything. I'm sure he meant well, but his theology just didn't hold up to the test we were going through.

God has proven to us time and again that what He desires from us is a personal relationship. He gives us divine connections as a means of showing His glory. Divine connections witness the reality of sensing God in the middle of it. He strategically places people in our path to bring encouragement and connect us to others that can help us fulfill our assignments. Sometimes those relationships are connected to new doors of opportunity.

The Holy Spirit was sent not just to empower believers but to personalize our relationship with our heavenly Father. It is the personal relationship with God that differentiates Christianity from any other religion. It is the fact that we learn to follow Him because of love and gratefulness that makes us different from other faiths, because Jesus Christ is the only true and *living* God.

He has promised in His word that He goes before us to prepare a place for us. He also sends an angel before us to lead the way. There are many examples in scripture on this subject, so we can receive His encouragement that he has also helped many of His servants on their journeys.

Jesus: "Don't get lost in despair; believe in God, and keep on believing in Me. My father's home is designed to accommodate all of you. If there were not room for everyone, I would have told you that. I am going to make arrangements for your arrival. I will be there to greet you personally and welcome you home, where we will be together. You know where I am going and how to get there."

Thomas: "Lord, we don't know where You are going, so how can we know the path?"

Jesus: "I am the path, the truth, and the energy of life. No one comes to the Father except through Me. If you know Me, you know the Father. Rest assured now; you have known Him and you have seen Him."

Philip: "Lord, all I am asking is that You show us the Father."

Jesus (to Philip): "I have lived with you all this time, and you still don't know who I am? If you have seen Me, you have seen the Father. How can you keep asking to see the Father? Don't you believe Me when I say I abide in the Father and the Father dwells in Me? I'm not making this up as I go along. The Father has given Me these truths that I have been speaking to you, and He empowers all My actions. Accept these truths: I am in the Father and the Father is in Me. If you have trouble based on My words, believe because of the things I have done."[7]

---

[7] John 14:1-12; The VOICE

CHAPTER 6

DOORS IN UNEXPECTED PLACES

God was faithful to continue to give Norm work. At first, it started out as a repair business, then grew into property management. God has unusual ways to present opportunities, and even when we are clueless, He has a way of propping a door open so that we don't miss the provision He has prepared for us.

Norm had done quite a lot of repair work for one particular condo complex, and his constant time spent at this place allowed him to get to know the resident manager. This man kept trying to get us to move into one of the units there, but we really had our heart set on a house, so we kept declining the offer. During this time we both got increasingly frustrated with where we were living. One day the offer presented itself again, and this time with a move-in special that made it really hard to say no, so we decided we would make the move. The evidence of God's peace was all over the place, and we knew it was a yes from the Lord.

Shortly thereafter, we learned that the resident manager was dying from cancer. A little at a time, Norm started helping him out simply as a courtesy, because he realized the man could not carry out certain duties. I began taking him some meals and helping out a little in the office. A few months later, as the manager was passing away, the owner of the complex showed up at our door unexpectedly. He asked if we would be interested in taking over the management responsibilities. The next day we met in his office to sign a formal agreement. I made the remark, "When we moved in we had no idea this would take place!" The owner looked at us with a little twinkle in his eye and said, "Well, Miles knew. He has been talking to me about the both of you for a year."

We were both so stunned! The place we had resisted moving into for a full year was the place God had purposed to bless us. When we weren't so quick to cooperate, He graciously held the door open. When an opportunistic person tried to grab that position for themselves, God kept it for us.

We learned a lot from that situation, too. First, the people we encounter will tell others about us, largely based on how we treat them. We can leave a good impression or a negative impression, but good impressions have the opportunity to open new and unexpected doors.

God has certain blessings marked out for every person. He knows every one of His kids by name. He knows what we're good at; our skill set, talents, experience and abilities. Whatever He has for us, is *for us*. We can take comfort in knowing that it doesn't belong to someone else, and He is not going to allow someone else to take what He has set aside as ours. He holds the keys to the doors in our life. He knows how to open doors and He knows how to close doors. He knows who is behind every door and who has the power to invite others through those doors.

One day we were driving home from out of town. We were driving down the coastal highway and all of a sudden there was a random door among all the shrubs. I am not sure what held it up, because it didn't seem to be attached to anything. There was literally nothing but shrubs on either side! There was no door frame and there didn't seem to be a house or structure; there was just this door with a house number on it. It was so odd and unexpected, but it occurred to me that sometimes that's how God works, too. He can put a door right where ever He chooses. It can be in front of us when we aren't even looking for one!

God delights in unconventional methods. He does not need to work within the familiarity of our past experiences. If a position doesn't exist where He wants to put us, He can create a new one. If someone is blocking the door or trying to shut us out of an opportunity God has for us, He can move them away from the door or get us through a different door. Sometimes He doesn't take you through the front door, because that's where the enemy is expecting you. Sometimes, in order to avoid tipping off a potential adversary or a jealous opponent, God will get you through a back door so that you come in unnoticed. The point is, our heavenly Father loves to create the solutions we need! We never need to feel insecure, jealous or competitive with others about potential opportunities, because if an opportunity is truly ours, God will save it for us. If God doesn't want it for us, then we shouldn't strive for it. It's never just about us, but about how He wants to use us to carry out some assignment. He knows how to maneuver us into position to fulfill His purposes.

Our Father is committed to helping us fulfill our destiny. Doors are opportunities, and every opportunity is connected to a person. Behind every door is a human heart. When you discover what moves the human heart, you have found a key that opens a door. If you discover where there is a need you can fill, you have found another key. Every door has a key that will open it, and if you use the right key, the door will open. Prayer is another key that opens doors, and so is worship. Ask God to help you see the opportunities in front of you. Ask Him for eyes to see new doors connected to opportunities in your everyday life. I have even heard stories of God putting a door in a place to supernaturally transport individuals from one place to another, sometimes even from one nation to another. He works in unusual ways all the time, so why do we doubt that He can help us find that new place where we're to live, or that new job, or arrange a divine connection with some key individual that is necessary for a new opportunity? He is skilled at putting doors in unusual places!

Many people struggle to make something work in a certain place with very little to show for it. If things aren't coming together where you are, you might ask the Lord to show you if He wants to move you somewhere else. God uses the things we consider unpredictable or random to direct us into something new. He also takes advantage of every opportunity, including the disasters of our life to propel us into change. Most people do not like change and will stay in a place that isn't healthy or productive until something dislodges them from their comfort zone. Change is often uncomfortable because it can bring a change in relationships, a new job, or even a new community. God uses people to open doors, and if our current social circles and other relationships aren't going to cause us to encounter the people He wants to use to bring us into the new thing He has for us, then God will orchestrate the change. He has to redirect us so that he can cause us to 'bump into' that destiny connection. There are certain people that are divine connections that can help us on the next leg of our journey.

"People do their best making plans for their lives, but the Eternal directs their steps." [8]

---

[8] Proverbs 16:9, The VOICE

CHAPTER 7

HIDDEN TREASURE

We had discussed moving into a larger home for several years, but it never seemed to be the right timing. We knocked on a few doors, but none opened. I grew increasingly frustrated over being cramped in too small of a space. The business had been doing well and things seemed to be stable for a reasonable period of time. That's not always easy to accomplish with a small business, especially for the self-employed. I couldn't figure out why we seemed to be stuck where we were, and God didn't seem to think he needed to fill me in on the details! It was a lesson in patience, and I learned the importance of attitude adjustments, gratitude and contentment.

Norm began working with a particular broker doing property management. The law required real estate agents to work under a broker for at least two years, and we were approached by a broker that had heard good things about Norm. It had been agreed upon ahead of time that whatever properties he brought in were his, and the properties that belonged to the broker before we came on board remained hers. We were doing most of the work, so we received the higher end of the income. Everything was going well for close to two years. We had built up the company and Norm had brought in a lot of his own properties. Then it gradually became apparent that the relationship was changing, but not for the better. The short version is that this broker ended up stealing our clients out from under us, leaving us high and dry. That in itself was another opportunity to practice forgiveness, and it wasn't easy. We had trusted the relationship but the contracts that had been signed between us protected the broker's interests, not ours. It felt terribly unfair, and it was. She hadn't worked for the properties Norm had brought in, but she was the one that continued to profit off of his labor.

The abrupt end to that relationship also brought an abrupt end to a sizable portion of our monthly income. We suffered an unexpected loss of income that was nearly $3,000 per month. One of the things we realized from that situation was the need to repent for putting our trust in other relationships as our source. We knew that, of course, but maybe somewhere along the line we had lost sight of that fact, because we felt that old familiar wave of insecurity sweep over us again. God will always be our source regardless of who He uses to help provide for us. Our Father saw all that coming, of course, and we realized that was why He hadn't opened a new door for us to move, but it still didn't answer the question as to how we were going to provide for our bills that month, or in the months afterward.

We were still managing the condos where we lived and those were under a different management company, so that was not affected by the situation with the broker, but that portion of our income was minimal. During the few months prior to us losing our properties, one of the apartments had been in court proceedings as an eviction due to being an abandoned unit. The family had left pretty much everything behind and we had no way to contact them. The apartment and their garage was full of their belongings. We posted the necessary notices and waited the appropriate amount of time that was required by law, then the management company told us to just get rid of the stuff because they didn't want to bother with it. At first glance, it certainly didn't look like there was anything of significant value. Once we opened the garage door, however, we discovered quite a few new things still in original packaging. There were so many boxes of stuff, it was like digging for treasure! Boxes within boxes, and we had to go through each one. All of a sudden I came to a box that contained many smaller jewelry boxes, and each one had gold jewelry in them. None of them by were very expensive pieces of jewelry, but when we started to get a pile of necklaces, earrings and gold charms, we realized they might be worth some money. The most surprising little envelope contained 7 gold Mexican coins.

We gathered up the jewelry and the coins and took them to a

place that bought gold. The gold coins were by far the most valuable items. We were shocked but happily surprised when it totaled over $2,000! Between the jewelry and the other things that were sold, it was enough to pay our bills.

You may have heard about another story a long, long time ago, involving Jesus and a fisherman named Peter. They had no money with which to pay their taxes. When Peter asked how they would pay what was owed, Jesus told Peter to go fishing. In other words, "Hey Peter! Go do what you know how to do best!" The provision supernaturally showed up as Peter obeyed His word. There was a gold coin in the mouth of the fish and they used it to pay their taxes. The Lord put that coin there to surprise Peter with the knowledge that He can create miracles of provision in the most astonishing places! We don't need to understand how He will accomplish the miracle we need; we need simply to believe that He will be faithful to take care of us and honor His promises.

Did Jesus put a gold coin in the mouth of the fish, or did He simply have foreknowledge of a coin that dropped into the water, knowing which fish gobbled it up? If God knows which fish would swallow a coin, doesn't it make sense that He also knows your every need? No matter how you choose to look at it, He still had to direct the fish to bite on Peter's hook! How many other men were fishing that day? How many other hooks did that fish have to swim past in order to get to Peter's line? We will never know!

Isn't it wonderful to realize how God takes precautions to prepare for emergency situations? His plan to provide for us must be accepted by faith, but it's when our Father's supply manifests that we realize the truth: what seemed like a sudden, unanticipated need in our life didn't go unnoticed by our dad! Long before we became aware there would be a need, Father made a note on his calendar to take care of it. Jesus put a gold coin in the mouth of a fish for Peter, and He put seven gold coins in a garage for us. It was like stumbling upon hidden treasure! The provision was there long before we needed it, waiting for the day we would discover it. It was planned long in advance by Someone who deeply cared for us. He transferred it into our hands when it was needed. Our Father's attention to detail is amazing and carefully thought out. It also demonstrates the practical application of how He fulfills the promise in Proverbs 13:22 that states, "the wealth of the sinner is stored up for the righteous." He knows how to transfer resources, food, finances or whatever is needed out of the hands of one person and into the hands of His children.

God's storehouses are everywhere, but it is faith in who He is that allows us to access the things that are stored up for us. When Jesus told Peter to go fishing, the thought that there would actually be a gold coin in a fish put there for him to find was an instruction that provoked awe and wonder. I can just see Peter rushing off down to the shore, eager to see the miracle with his own eyes! He had been around Jesus long enough to understand that when He was around, out of the ordinary happenings occurred. Peter's curiosity was stirred as he went in search of the supernatural, but he didn't put his faith in the fish. It was faith in the person he had come to know that caused the sign to appear. Jesus's words always came to pass. If He said it, it was as good as done.

Jesus said, "…go down to the lake, cast a hook, and pull in the first fish that bites. Open your mouth and you'll find a coin. Take it and give it to the tax men. It will be enough for both of us."[9]

---

[9] Matthew 17:24-27, Message Bible

CHAPTER 8
ACCESSING GOD'S STRATEGIES

Life gives us plenty of opportunities to test our character. How we respond to the unexpected determines the duration of those tests, but those seasons don't last forever. We endured long periods of having our faith stretched, situations that tested our integrity level and our ability to forgive the unjust treatment from others. For the longest time, it felt as though we kept hitting an invisible wall. We would make some progress only to encounter set back after set back. It became very disheartening.

Losing the majority of our property management business was hard to deal with, but at the same time we thanked God for separating us from someone that lacked integrity. In all the years of self-employment there were a couple of situations where God clearly delivered us from being yoked with the wrong people. The first person had a serious anger issue, and the second one, a lack of ethics and moral character.

Once again we found ourselves facing a situation where we needed to start over, but how – and with what? We lacked finances, direction and clarity. One day we were sitting out by the community pool when a friend and neighbor began to tell us about starting up his own business. He told Norm about getting his contractor's license, and encouraged Norm to do the same. He even offered to give us his books so that Norm could study for the exam.

Norm was very busy trying to work twice as hard to make up for the lost income. It didn't seem very practical for him to try to add more to his plate, and we continued to pray. When our friend mentioned the books to Norm a second time, he decided to take Mark up on his offer. While I was trying to hear God speak, Norm was looking for signs. God speaks through natural signs that indicate He is leading a particular direction. Do you remember playing that old guessing game called 'I Spy' when you were a kid? The first spy would pick an object and then have to give clues until the other players could figure out what he or she had chosen. The first spy would give little clues by saying, "You're getting warmer," if you moved towards the correct object, or they would say, "You're getting colder," if you moved in the wrong direction. Sometimes I think that's how God leads us, too! We have to look for the signs that seem to point to the same direction.

When our friend suggested taking the contractor's exam and he gave Norm the books for it, that saved us over $500. It was clearly a sign pointing us in a new direction. It was hard for Norm to make time to study after working all day but he took the test and passed. Before the contractor board could post his new license number on their website, Mark was at the door letting Norm know that he had a potential contract waiting for him, but it all hinged on him having that contractor license number. Finally the day came when Norm's license number was issued, and that same day Mark stopped by again with a contract in hand for Norm to sign. He also introduced Norm to some new key relationships at a particular company that led to a generous supply of work. The opportunities literally hunted us down and threw themselves in our lap!

During all the time we were frustrated and feeling stuck, we had no idea God had arranged a divine connection literally right across the street. If we had tried to force a door open to leave prematurely, we would have missed that important connection – AND thousands of dollars in new work! I thanked God He didn't allow us to leave before we encountered the blessing! If you feel stuck but don't know why, ask God to give you that divine connection that will get things moving again or ask Him to give you the prayers to help move the situation along. Sometimes it's not about you, but about something going on in someone else's life, a door they need to go through, or a situation that needs to occur to make room for you.

Getting the contractor's license was the key that opened new doors. An abundance of work came pouring in from different places. About 9 months later, another wonderful opportunity showed up unexpectedly, and we were able to move into a beautiful home. That, too, was through another personal connection. God has times and seasons for pruning, loss, testing and growing our faith, but He also has seasons for restoration. You just never know when that day will suddenly appear! No matter what you're going through, hold on to God through it, because you are one day closer to the end of the old season.

God has been giving people strategies for success for many years, and He is good at it! He wants to help us. Let me shift your attention to a person in the Bible that received God's strategy for business. His name was Jacob, and you can find his story in the Book of Genesis. Jacob started out as someone who didn't always have integrity, but there were many years where Jacob got a taste of his own medicine. He reaped what he sowed, but in the process of time those things served to humble him and change his nature. Jacob went to work for a man named Laban, who was notorious for changing his wages on a frequent basis, and generally quite crafty at devising ways to take advantage of Jacob. Laban was also Jacob's father-in-law, but he was just as manipulative and deceptive as Jacob! Both men seemed to contrive ways to get the better of one another, but Jacob found himself fulfilling a contract that continually left him on the short end of the stick.

Jacob's skills as a shepherd caused Laban to become quite wealthy, but Jacob became quite frustrated being stuck in a situation where he could never prosper. Although scripture doesn't say that Jacob prayed for wisdom, scripture gives other references of Jacob calling out to God, so it makes sense that he sought God's help for the problems he had with Laban, too. He was the son of Isaac, Abraham's promised child. Both Jacob's father and grandfather were wealthy, successful men, and they were men that walked with God.

Jacob was a son of God, but that wasn't true about Laban. Laban possessed many idols and worshipped a variety of gods. This is important because Laban had no relationship with God; therefore, God was not obligated to Laban. God is not duty-bound to hear and respond to those that have no relationship with Him. The promises of God are intended for those that welcome Him into their life and make a commitment to know Him.

One night Jacob had a dream, and it was the dream that revealed wisdom for success. In the dream, an angel called Jacob's name and told him to pay attention to what he saw. As it turned out, it was God's strategy for prosperity. The angel told Jacob that God had seen the injustice in how Laban had treated him, and He was giving him a way out of his predicament. Jacob took the information revealed from his dream and put it into practice. It was a way to breed the goats and increase the striped, speckled and spotted animals that were his split of the flock. Jacob's portion of the flock also grew healthier and stronger. In time, Jacob's flock outgrew Laban's and caused him to prosper so that he could break free from Laban's control.

God diminished Laban's flock because it was gained through dishonesty (a Biblical principle found in Proverbs 13:11), and it was given over to Jacob, who by this time had gone through some personal transformation. Laban was shrewd, but he wasn't wise. If he was wise, he would have inquired and wanted to know the God that prospered Jacob. Laban understood that he was getting blessed because of Jacob's God and didn't want him to leave; not because he wanted to know the God who fought for His people, but because he wanted the financial increase to remain in his house. God will not be used like some talisman for good luck. He wants to prosper His children, but He also knows what motivates people. He knows if the love of money is our treasure or if our heart desires Him. We have to make sure our priorities are in the right place. One of those priorities is to ask for wisdom. Don't pray for wealth; pray for wisdom. Wealth never goes away, it just changes hands. God has purposed that His children can partner with Him to reap the benefits of success including the transfer of wealth, but no one can do it without wisdom.

We can access the strategies of God by coming into His presence. Sometimes people receive direction, wisdom and strategies through dreams, like Jacob. At other times, it may be through time spent in worship. Linger in His presence until you get an inspired thought or directive from the Lord. Gather together with others that have a prophetic anointing, and pray with people to help you hear what God is saying about your situation. Ask Him to confirm His word to you. These are ways to access the wisdom to direct important decisions. We can all benefit from having prophetic and apostolic people in our lives. The prophetic gift accesses what God is saying, while the apostolic anointing understands how to implement it. True success can come in any area of life if we will bring the gifts of the Holy Spirit into our circumstances. The wisdom of God will help lead you into blessing, restoration and prosperity. As our soul prospers, so will the rest of our life!

"I would have lost heart unless I believed I would see the goodness of God in the land of the living."[10]

---

[10] Psalm 27:13, NKJV

CHAPTER 9
SHATTERING RELIGIOUS MISCONCEPTIONS

One thing we discovered on our journey is that God is not nearly as religious as we had been led to believe. Religiousness has always made demands and stipulations on how to earn God's blessing and generosity. Over the years we had heard messages declaring the many reasons why a person wouldn't be blessed by God, but the God we experienced was not the God of religion. Our experience led us to discover the love, mercy and grace of a Father that loves us and desires to provide for us; not because we are perfect, but because we are His.

If God's generosity towards us is measured by our works then His love, grace and mercy are also measured by our works. The Holy Spirit was given to us to personalize our relationship with God. It can be easy to make Christianity simply about doing 'business as usual.' What I mean by that is when people live their Christian life doing things out of obligation or a sense of responsibility rather than personal relationship with Christ. When a person does things because they think that's what's expected of them, that's being dutiful. Of course we need to honor our commitments and demonstrate responsibility, but God is not just after a sense of duty. He's looking for people who truly know Him and walk in relationship with Him. God is looking for actions birthed out of a love for Him and others. Religious traditions and obligations should not become a replacement for relationship with God.

When we pray, prayer should not just be about taking care of business but about conversation. Conversation involves listening, understanding the other person's heart and their point of view. The other person's feelings and perspective are equally important to the relationship. The dialog that results from this personal relationship comes from a place of truly knowing how the other person feels about certain things. When we speak, we share what's on our heart, but prayer also involves representing God's heart in our petitions. The journey in each person's life is designed to create opportunities where we gain a deeper sense of understanding God's ways, because when we learn His ways, we can then understand His heart. Personal experiences with God are what reveal His consistent love, provision, care and concern. The revelation we gain does not come by religious traditions taught by men, but by knowing Him through experience. Experience is something no one can ever take from us! These things lay the foundation of trust in our relationship with God, built upon the revelation of Jesus Christ. All of this has been given to us to help us know a gracious, compassionate Father.

During transition we were not always in a church; therefore, our giving did not meet religious requirements, but we encountered opportunities to bless others wherever God led us. There are always opportunities to be a blessing to others whether it's through prayer or helping to meet some practical need. He is not looking for people that will give robotically or out of a sense needing to fulfill some religious duty, but people that will be kind and generous to others. Tithing is dutiful, and God promises windows of heaven will pour out blessing if people tithe, but giving because we have a spirit of generosity supersedes the minimum requirements of religious duty.

There was a man named Cornelius in Acts chapter 10 that was described as a godly man, reverent and a generous giver. His compassion for others was reflected in his giving and it got heaven's attention. God wanted to bless Cornelius with something that money couldn't buy: *salvation*. Cornelius was a good man, but lacked understanding of the revelation that would pull him into a personal relationship with God, so the Father sent angels to his house to arrange a divine connection with a man (Peter) that would explain the gospel message o Cornelius. Cornelius' generosity became a direct path to his salvation! That was a far greater reward than financial gain.

There is a blessing and a promise to us whether we tithe or

whether we give out of compassion and generosity, but it always comes down to the condition of a person's heart. A person's giving is directly controlled by their fears, insecurities, whether or not they trust God to provide for them, areas of selfishness, and compassion towards others. When we go to bless someone, we don't ask if they're a tither or question them as to their giving habits. Our desire to bless someone is not contingent upon whether they are a giver, but because Holy Spirit moved on our hearts to do something for them.

A religious spirit will try to take our liberty and bring it back into captivity. No one is justified by the works of the law, and that applies to giving as well as other aspects of trying to adhere to the law. Joy, peace and freedom is available through the Spirit of God. In chapter 3 in the Book of Galatians, the Apostle Paul pointed out that the foundation of being in right relationship with God had everything to do with his relationship with the Spirit of God. He pointed out that the Holy Spirit had been at work in those considered 'outsiders.' Therefore, they weren't really 'outsiders' at all, but absolutely included as part of God's family. "You have experienced the Spirit He gave you in powerful ways. Miracle after miracle has occurred right before your eyes in this community, so tell me: did all this happen because you have kept certain provisions of God's law, or was it because you heard the gospel and accepted it by faith?"[11]

We believe in giving and supporting the local church, but we

---

[11] Galatians 3:5 The VOICE

also don't want people to feel condemned if they are not a part of one, and we don't want people to walk in fear in regards to provision.

When there are bills to pay and children to feed, it's not always easy to give away finances. Fear and insecurity about whether or not a person will have enough can cause a wrestling match between the soul and spirit. It is God's will to have His children understand what it means to have a generous heart. That is one reason why He is not miserly with us. A parent instructs a child through their own conduct. It would be hypocritical for God to expect something from us that He is not willing to give us, and He is not a hypocrite. How can we learn to be generous unless He demonstrates generosity to us? His faithfulness to His own character means that He cannot deny who He is, and God's compassion, generosity and love compels Him to bless us.

Apostle Paul taught so many things on cultivating a generous spirit. Paul wanted people to understand God's generosity, too. He knew that giving was directly related to a heart condition, and he wanted others to understand the importance of becoming a vessel of blessing. It was this same generous spirit that caused the gospel to flourish. In the book of Acts, people fellowshipped with one another, prayed for each other, and helped provide for each other's needs. It was compassion through generosity that demonstrated the authenticity of God's spirit moving among them. Love compelled people to trust God for their salvation, and it propelled the gospel to spread into new locations.

God has the blueprints for our life. He knows what is on the road ahead and has made provision ready. Sometimes we need a blessing and other times we are the ones that can help meet someone else's need. Through it all, His purpose has been constant: to give us a kingdom that cannot be shaken. If we do what we can to practice being a blessing to others, God will continue to supply to us. That is a spiritual principle of His kingdom. We are blessed to be a blessing!

There can be many things that trigger an intervention from God. Sacrifice, generosity, and creating a lifestyle of giving are key principles in the kingdom of heaven. Praise and worship open doors. Prayer and declaring God's word are also powerful and effective weapons. May you prosper in every aspect of your heart and life!

"Giving grows out of the heart. Otherwise, you've reluctantly grumbled "yes," because you felt you had to or you couldn't say "no," but this isn't the way God wants it. For we know that God loves a cheerful giver. God is ready to overwhelm you with more blessings than you could ever imagine so that you'll always be taken care of in every way and you'll have more than enough to share."[12] "The same One that has put seed into the hands of the sower and brought bread to fill our stomachs will provide and multiply the

---

[12] 2 Corinthians 9:7,8

resources you invest and produce an abundant harvest from your righteous actions."[13]

---

[13] 2 Corinthians 9:10,11

CHAPTER 10
PRAYERS AND DECLARATIONS FOR FINANCIAL RESTORATION

Father God,

You want us to prosper, but You also want our souls to prosper.
I repent for any wrong attitudes and actions that demonstrate selfishness, worry, fear, complaining or doubt. I know that those things do not please you and they do not demonstrate faith. I am grateful, Lord, for my home, my family, and all that you have given to bless my life. I am grateful for You, Lord Jesus. Thank you for being my Savior. Thank you for your love, acceptance and the forgiveness of my sins.

I ask You to forgive my sins and those in my family line. Forgive us for the sins of idolatry, rebellion, and self-will. Forgive us for any involvement in the occult and for allowing other influences to govern our ways. I renounce all unholy alliances and ungodly covenants that have been made knowingly or unknowingly. I renounce any old contracts and covenants between myself, my ancestors and the enemy that have given the enemy legal grounds to enforce them. Let the blood of Jesus cover those sins, contracts and covenants. Please let the blood of Jesus cover those sins.

I pray for myself and others, that they would also receive You as their Lord and Savior, and receive Your help. For those that need jobs, please help them get hired at a good job. For those that need their health restored, please heal them. For those that need specific things, please meet their needs over and above what they need. Let them be very blessed, and if anyone is holding onto unforgiveness, please help them to forgive so that You can forgive their sins, too.

Father, as a child of God, I submit to You and resist the works of the devil. I resist the spirits of fear and insecurity. I resist the spirit of accusation that wants to lie to me and tell me that You will not take care of me. I choose to trust that You are faithful, even though I may experience things that cause me to be uncomfortable and unsettled.

I take authority over poverty and death, and forbid these thieving spirits of death and hell from advancing against me, my family and my livelihood. I tell them all, "Be bound, In Jesus name." According to what Jesus has already done on the cross, I command these spirits to be silent, impotent, and void of any and all power. Leave me now, in Jesus name.

I speak to all demonic dams that have held back my blessings, opportunities and open doors. I command all demonic dams to come apart, be struck down, and release that which has been stored up for me.

I thank You, Father that the favor of God surrounds me like a shield according to Psalm 5:12. I thank You for the blessings, finances, divine connections, and blueprints for success that are rightfully mine. I call forth raises, promotions, retroactive compensation, new contracts for business and everything hidden by the enemy. Let them come forth, make themselves known, and be put into my hands in Jesus name.

I release the Holy Spirit, the Spirit of Truth, to show me any areas of my life that may be hindering me from receiving increase in blessing and prosperity. If I need to be realigned in some way, show me. If there are relational changes that need to take place, please help make those divine connections. Forgive me, Lord, for areas of my heart and life that represent selfishness and greed. Give me a generous spirit towards blessing others. Let the work of my hands be blessed. Let fruitfulness and increase be released in my family.

I command all illegal encroachers, both in the natural and spiritual to be removed from that which concerns me and my family. Please let angelic assistance be released to help remove any spiritual hindrances to breakthrough.

Let blessing and favor be released over my employment, business contacts and finances. I command the enemy to restore everything he has taken, according to Proverbs 6:31, and with a 7-fold increase. I command all mountains of resistance to be removed, every gate unlocked, and every door that is connected to Your opportunities to be opened. In Jesus name, Amen.

Prayer to Heal the Land, Family & Business

Dear Heavenly Father,

I come before you to ask for Your protection and blessing upon my home, family and business. I ask for healing on the land where my home and business are located. If any previous landowners sinned and never asked You for forgiveness, I come to You now to identify with their sins and ask You for mercy and forgiveness so that this land and everything on it may receive Your blessing.

On behalf of myself, anyone in my generational line and previous landowners, I repent and ask You to forgive the sins of idolatry and rebellion. I renounce any and all ungodly oaths and covenants that were made including those with secret societies. I break all agreements and renounce any covenants or involvement with: the occult, demonic spirits, rituals and traditions that involve the use of idols, witchcraft; conjuring, and the use of mediums, familiar spirits, and witch doctors. In the name and authority of the Lord Jesus Christ, I cancel any contracts, covenants and alliances that have provided the enemy with legal rights to this land, home, business and our family.

Forgive me and those in my family line of practicing witchcraft and magic, shedding innocent blood, invoking demonic spirits and the worship of false gods and idols. I command all ungodly altars to be silent, torn down and familiar spirits to be severed from demonic thrones both in the earthly and heavenly realm.

Lord, let there be a release and a cancellation of every curse that has come as a result of these things. Let all demonic attachments be severed from myself, my family line and that which concerns my business.

Forgive me, my family line, and all previous landowners for any sins involving the abuse of trust, authority, power or using our influence in an ungodly manner.

Now Father, as I have made these renouncements and declarations, I command the enemy and every illegal encroacher (in the spiritual and in the natural realm) off the land in Jesus name. I have legal rights to the land by the contracts I have signed, therefore, I command the enemy to take everything he has brought into this place to be gone immediately in Jesus name.

Poverty, death, hell, sickness, disease and all manner of curses - GO NOW. Torment, mental illness, unbelief, misery - GO! I command all works of evil to cease immediately, and I ask You Father to set a hedge of protection around me, my family and this business. I declare that poverty, infirmity, death, hell and all that comes from the evil one will not prosper against me, my family or my business from this moment on. We belong to the Lord Jesus Christ and declare Jesus is Lord over all that concerns us.

Father, You gave me a promise even as You gave it to Your servant Joshua many years ago. You said everywhere I put my foot has already been given to me and so I claim that victory and right of inheritance for me, my family and the kingdom of God. Let Your kingdom come and Your will be done in my home, my life, my family and in this business. I declare blessings to come forth. I speak blessing, increase, favor over my family and over all who enter these premises. I ask for Divine Connections and sensitivity to Your Spirit. Let me be an agent of healing, grace, love and encouragement to all who grace this place with their presence. In Jesus name, amen.

Prayer and Declaration for Business Owners

Almighty God,

I invite you, Lord Jesus, into my heart and life to be my Lord and Savior, and I thank You for your forgiveness. I ask Your forgiveness for any wrong doing committed by myself, business partners, landlords and landowners upon which my business resides. Let me be released from any ungodly oaths or covenants that have been made without Your approval. Let every generational curse be broken now and the blood of Jesus cover those sins.

I know that I am in need of godly wisdom, strategy and counsel in order to conduct my business in such a way that I can be a blessing to my family and others. I invite You, O God, to be my business partner and show me how to prosper. I eagerly desire Your blessing and favor upon my home, family and business. Therefore, as a business owner in this city, I declare that I will persevere to conduct my affairs with good character, while upholding honesty, integrity and loyalty to those I serve.

I declare that mercy and truth are a trademark of my life and business. (Proverbs 3:3; Prov. 16:16)

I declare that I am blessed with creative ideas that are anointed for breakthrough. (Prov. 8:12)

I declare that Holy Spirit has given me strategies for success. (Prov. 16:3; Jer. 29:11; Amos 3:7; Prov. 3:5)

I declare that I am endowed with inner strength, conviction and courage to avoid temptations that would lead me into the wrong things. (John 16:13; Joshua 1:7-9; Is. 41:10-13; Luke 22:40; Matt. 6:13)

I declare that I am filled with godly wisdom to know how to implement new ideas. (James 1:5,6)

I declare that You will guide me to make any changes that are needed, including the best location so that my business will prosper. (Gen. 24:27; Acts 7:46; John 16:13)

I declare that You will help me correctly identify people's needs and how to offer the products that benefit my customer's needs. (Ps. 119:66; Ps. 119:130; Col. 4:6; Prov. 4:7; Prov. 20:5)

'I declare Holy Spirit counsels me with wisdom that outwits my competitors. (Phil. 4:19: Mathew 6:33; Luke 21:15; 2 Tim. 2:7)

I declare blessing and favor will overtake me and cause me to inherit the goodness of God. (Gen. 6:8; Gen. 39:21)

I declare that the favor of God supernaturally directs people to my business. (Ps. 5:12; Prov. 3:4; Jer. 32:41)

I declare an increase in divine encounters, sales and contracts that increase my business.(Prov. 12:2; Numbers 6:25; Ps. 67:1)

I declare my business is blessed to be a blessing to others and is an testimony of God's goodness in my life. (Gen. 12:2) Thank You, Father, for hearing this prayer and declaration and sending forth Your answers. In Jesus name, Amen.

Prayer for Wisdom

Father God,

I ask You for wisdom to know how to correctly handle any situation I may encounter. I need wisdom and strategy in order to be successful in my future, and even just in my daily life with my family, work and personal relationships.

I also ask You for strategy to succeed in business, sensitivity to Your Spirit, to know how to correctly understand what You're communicating, and a heart that is quick to obey You.

I ask You for wisdom to know what to do and how to manage whatever success You allow me to have. I acknowledge it is You that gives me power to gain wealth, Lord. Help me to have the quality of character that pleases You so that I can be a blessing to others.

I ask You to increase my faith so that I will not shrink back when You require a taking a great risk. Show me how to prosper Your way, Lord Jesus. I thank You for helping me pay attention to your signs and walk into the newness of whatever You have planned for me. In Jesus name, amen.

Prayer to be Healed from Emotional Trauma

Dear Heavenly Father,

I pray that You would help me embrace whatever traumatic or negative memories that I have either blocked out or forgotten. I do not have to fear any negative memory for You are with me. You have said that You will never leave me, therefore I am safe in your care. I give You permission to dislodge memories that are stuck.

Show me where I have partnered with lies. I invite your Holy Spirit to speak to me. Reveal what I currently believe about past situations and expose the lies, so that the power of the past is broken. I pray that You highlight any specific memories or situations that are related to fear, trust issues, and lies that I have believed about You. Help me pay attention to what You show me. Please give me understanding of what was going on in myself and others connected to those events, and grant me grace and compassion to be able to forgive myself and others. Help me to see from Your perspective so that the truth can make me free.

I pray that You would supernaturally remove the hurtful memories and the trauma of past events out of my emotions and thought processes. I ask that You would remove the trauma that was created as a result of pain. Lift it all out of the very cells of my body.

Let me remember only the good about those the enemy used to cause pain. I pray that my heart and mind would agree that I am in an entirely new day and I am able to graciously forgive those that treated me wrong. I forgive anyone that caused physical injury to me, including wounding to my soul, now Lord, help me to pray blessing over them and set my heart free.

I forgive and release those who willfully and spitefully inflicted pain and suffering on me. I forgive and release those who had wicked intentions and gave themselves over to evil, in order to afflict, torment, and delight themselves in causing me pain.

Let my ears not remember hurtful words spoken to me, about me, by me, or by others. Let my heart release all unforgiveness, anger, fear, rejection, pain and shame. I declare that painful memories and hurtful words will not circulate in my mind and emotions any longer in the name and authority of Jesus Christ.

I release myself and others from the pain of their past, and the poor decisions they made as a result of their brokenness. I release them from guilt, shame, regret and bitterness in Jesus name.. I give them over to You, Father, to do with as You choose; knowing that You are a just God. I choose to forgive and am therefore free in Christ. Please allow my heart to witness the truth of these statements.

I ask Your forgiveness for any doors that I have accidentally opened to the enemy through trying to comfort myself with artificial means. I renounce and break every unintentional agreement that I may have made with spirits of fear, lust, anger, greed, gluttony, anger, bitterness, unforgiveness, unloving spirits, idolatry or a perverse spirit that also inflicts wounds on others.

I renounce the lies that have told me that You are insensitive, uncaring or disinterested in me, and have made room for a spirit of distortion to operate in my life.

I renounce the lies that my Father is harsh, hard to please, stern and demanding according to Zeph. 3:17 and Romans 15:7

I renounce the lies that You are displeased with who I am as a person and have rejected me, for I am accepted in the Beloved according to Ephesians 1:6.

I renounce the lies that You are condemning and unforgiving, according to Psalm 130:1-4 and Luke 15:17-24. Your word tells me that You came into the world to save it, not to condemn it.

I renounce the lies that I must be performance oriented. I thank You that You do not demand perfection from me. Rom. 8:28-29, Heb. 12:5-11 and 2 Cor. 7:4.

I renounce the lie that I am unimportant or insignificant, for You sent Your only Son to die for me. I AM important to You! You also said you would freely give me all things because of Your great love according to Romans 8:32 and Deuteronomy 32:9-10.

I renounce the lie that I cannot hear from God or know Your thoughts towards me for Your word is a lamp to my feet and a light onto my path, according to Psalm 119:105.

I declare I am blessed because You are kind, compassionate, intimate and involved in my life, according to Psalm 103:8-14 and Psalm 139:1-18

I declare that You are always with me, and You are delighted in me according to Hebrews 13:5 and Jer. 31:20.

I declare that I am blessed because You are trustworthy and you want to give me a full life according to John 10:10.

I declare that I know Your good, perfect and acceptable will for my life according to Lamentations 3:22-23, and Romans 12:2

I submit to You, Holy Spirit, and command all ungodly spirits to leave me now, in the name and authority of Jesus Christ. I command all unclean spirits to go back to where they came from and I appropriate the blood of Christ over every part of my life.

Let every weight be released. Let every hindrance be released. Holy Spirit, fill me now with Your fullness, strength and power in Jesus name. Fill me with joy, peace, and a release of supernatural healing that radiates from the inside out.

I thank You for pulling out the roots of bitterness, offense, anger and unforgiveness and planting love, peace, joy and generosity in their place.

I thank You for spoiling the plans of the enemy that were set against me and bringing recompense.

I thank You for correcting my spiritual vision and understanding of You, and helping me to see Your purposes along my journey.

I thank You that I no longer view myself as unworthy, unloved, rejected or abandoned.

I declare that by Your stripes I have been healed, according to Is. 53:5. Thank you for the blood You shed, Lord Jesus, that makes healing a reality. I thank You for revival, restoration and healing in Jesus name. Amen.

Prayer for God's Intervention

Father,

I thank You that creating the miracle I need is a simple thing for You. Forgive me for putting my confidence in the wrong things, and for taking my eyes off of You. I shake off unbelief and I thank You that You surround me with favor as a shield. According to Psalm 5:12.

I thank You that you compel others to step in and help me. I thank You that You influence people to help make dreams, desires and prayers become realities, according to Psalm 37:3,4.

I thank You that You provide for me out of Your goodness, and it is Your deep desire to make me whole in every way, according to Philippians 4:19, Psalm 84:11.

I thank You for finding what's been lost, taken unlawfully and plundered, and for catching the thief according to Prov. 6:31.

I thank You for releasing the judgement in my favor, sending out the answer to prayer and restoring the losses of previous years. You are a great restorer, and I thank You for pouring out the blessings that will make my heart leap for joy. In Jesus name, Amen.

AUTHOR BIO

Laura Gagnon is blessed with the gift of understanding God's restorative work through her own personal experiences. She knows first-hand the power of God's compassion, grace and mercy. Through her prophetic insights, teaching and revelation, God has led her to influence many people into a restored relationship with Jesus Christ. Once bound by bitterness, witchcraft, lust, shame and fear, she now helps others find their way out of spiritual oppression. Laura stands on the promises of God and encourages others in an elevated expectation of the miraculous, boldly declaring the gift of His life. Laura has authored other books including ***Healing the Heart of a Woman, Prayers for Impossible Situations, Seduced into Shame and Healing the Heart of a Nation.*** She is co-author of her husband's book, ***Room to Grow***, and also writes for her blog, "Beyond the Barriers." Contact Laura Gagnon at xpectamiracle@yahoo.com.

Manufactured by Amazon.ca
Bolton, ON